The
Idea
of
Police

D1738356

LAW AND CRIMINAL JUSTICE SERIES
Series Editor: James A. Inciardi
Division of Criminal Justice, University of Delaware

The **Law and Criminal Justice Series** provides students in criminal justice, criminology, law, sociology, and related fields with a set of short textbooks on major topics and subareas of the field. The texts range from books that introduce the basic elements of criminal justice for lower division under-graduates to more advanced topics of current interest for advanced under-graduates and beginning graduate students. Each text is concise, didactic, and produced in an inexpensive paperback as well as hardcover format. Each author addresses the major issues and areas of current concern in that topic area, reporting on and synthesizing major research done on the subject. Case examples, chapter summaries, and discussion questions are generally included in each volume to aid in classroom use. The modular format of the series provides attractive alternatives to large, expensive classroom textbooks or timely supplements to more traditional class materials.

Volumes in this series:

Additional volumes currently in development.

The Idea of Police

CARL B. KLOCKARS

Volume 3.
Law and Criminal Justice Series

 SAGE PUBLICATIONS Beverly Hills London New Delhi

For information address:

SAGE Publications, Inc.
275 South Beverly Drive
Beverly Hills, California 90212

SAGE Publications India Pvt. Ltd.
C-236 Defence Colony
New Delhi 110 024, India

SAGE Publications Ltd
28 Banner Street
London EC1Y 8QE, England

Printed in the United States of America

Library of Congress Cataloging in Publication Data

Klockars, Carl B.
    The idea of police.

    (Law and criminal justice series ; v. 3)
    Includes index.
    1. Police. 2. Police patrol. 3. Detectives.
4. Law enforcement. I. Title. II. Series.
HV7921.K59   1985   363.2   84-26205
ISBN 0-8039-2178-0
ISBN 0-8039-2179-9 (pbk.)

FIRST PRINTING

CONTENTS

ABOUT THE AUTHOR

CARL B. KLOCKARS is Associate Professor of Criminal Justice at the University of Delaware. He received his Ph.D. in sociology from the University of Pennsylvania in 1973. Dr. Klockars is the author or editor of three books: *The Professional Fence, Deviance and Decency* (with Finbarr O'Connor), and *Thinking About Police.* He has also written extensively about professional and white-collar crime, criminological research ethics, criminological theory, criminal investigation, and qualitative methodology.

1

THE IDEA OF POLICE

When I teach my introductory course on police, I begin the first lecture by asking my students to take a sheet of paper from their notebooks and write down a definition of "police." I tell them to think carefully about what they write because in three minutes I will select a few of them to read their definitions to the class. I would ask you to do the same, but I have read enough books myself to know that if I did you would not do so. You would merely look ahead to the next paragraphs of this book to find out what I was going to say about definitions of police.

Fair enough. But for reasons you cannot yet appreciate, it is imporant for you to begin your study of police by thinking through the problem of defining it. So let me start you thinking with some of the more interesting definitions I have managed to force from my students:

> The police are a body of handsome young men and women, like Eric Estrada and Angie Dickenson, who bravely fight the forces of evil to make the world safe for decent people. [This definition was offered by a handsome and humorous young man who worked for the campus police.]

> The police are a bunch of hot shots who get their kicks from hassling blacks, students, and most other people who are trying to have a good time. [This definition is the effort of a tall, thin, hairy fellow with a widely advertised appetite for controlled substances.]

> The police are an agency of government which enforces the law and keeps the peace. [This one came from a very serious young woman who always sat in the front row. She remembered it from another class.]

The police are a weapon the state uses to oppress the working classes, the poor, and minorities. [The author of this definition was an intense young Marxist.]

The police are the people who come into my father's restaurant to get free food. [This from a second-generation Eastern European student.]

The police are the people who drive police cars. [The effort of one of the brightest students I have ever taught. She went on to become a lawyer.]

NORM-DERIVATIVE DEFINITIONS
OF "POLICE"

What do all these very different attempts at defining "police" have in common? First, all of them are at least partly true. Some police do drive police cars; some get free food, hassle poor folks, keep peace, and enforce laws. Some even sport an Angie Dickenson/Eric Estrada-class appearance.

Second, all of them are at least partly false. It is obvious that most pople do not look like Angie or Eric, and, of course, there were police before there were police cars. Some don't take free food from restaurants and others don't hassle students, the poor, or minorities. There are many laws the police hardly ever enforce, and anyone even remotely familiar with police history can point to numerous occasions on which police have not only failed to keep the peace but profoundly disturbed it as well.

Third, all of these definitions (and, chances are, the one you would have written if I could have got you to write one) are what sociologists call "norm-derivative." That is, they are definitions based on beliefs about what police *should* do or are *supposed* to be, about the *purposes* or *ends* of policing. This is true even of those definitions above that are critical of police. It is precisely because the author of a critical definition believes police should do or be something else that makes critical definitions possible.

The curious thing about all of the above definitions, all of which try to define police in terms of what they are supposed to do, is that they end up telling us more about the author of the definition, what he or she wants or expects police to do or be, than about police. This is a very important problem for anyone who wants to create an objective definition of police. No definition of police will do if it is merely a reflection of the hopes, desires, fears, frustrations, politics, or sense of humor of its author. And any norm-derivative definition of police—any definition of police that tries to define it in terms of its *ends*—will ultimately amount to nothing more than that.

Building a Definition of Police

"Police" cannot be satisfactorily defined in terms of its *ends*. A proper definition of it must be based on its *means*. That is, it must be based on the fundamental tool police use to do their work rather than on what they use that tool to do. The reason for this is that throughout history, in this country and elsewhere, the police have used the means that defines them to achieve so many different ends that no ends-based definition could possibly define them.

So, if we wish to build a definition of police based on means rather than ends, what means should we choose? It must be a means common to all police everywhere and at all times. It would not do to have a definition of police that defined only American police, Italian police, or German police; nor would it do to have our definition apply only to police of this century. Thus the means on which we choose to base our definition of police must be truly universal. It must be a means common to every police that has ever existed. Moreover, it must be a means that distinguishes police, as far as possible, from other groups and individuals who may use that means as well. What means is it that all police everywhere and at all times have claimed a right to use? What means is it that distinguishes police in their special right to use it?

The answer is *coercive force*.[1] No police anywhere has ever existed, nor it is possible to conceive of a genuine police ever existing, that does not claim a right to compel other people forcibly to do something. If it did not claim such a right, it would not be a police.

Having said this much about the means common to all police, we could define police as follows:

Individuals or institutions who claim a right to use coercive force.

This definition is absolutely true of all police. But, of course, the problem with it is that it is also true of all sorts of other groups and individuals: bank robbers, parents, the military, prize fighters, football players, prison guards, and schoolteachers, to name a few. All of them also claim the right to use coercive force under certain conditions. So although we are on the right track with our definition insofar as it defines all police, we must modify it to exclude all sorts of other groups and individuals who are not police.

The Police and The Bank Robber: The State's Monopoly. Let's first take up the problem of distinguishing the police right to use coercive force from the bank robber's right to use it. You might well respond to that "problem" by saying that it is no problem at all. Bank robbers do not have a right to use coercive force. You would be right, of course, but only if you specified that the only institution in modern society that can grant a legitimate right to use coercive force is the state.[2]

It must, however, be added that at times in early history states were not the only institutions with the right to grant legitimacy to the use of coercive force. At those times the church, the family, the tribe, the clan, and other institutions that were as powerful or, in some cases, more powerful than the state itself could and did confer, independent of the state, legitimate rights to use coercive force. In fact, it is only when a state gains a *monopoly* on the right to legitimate the use of coercive force (i.e., that the state becomes the *only* place one can go to receive such a right or have it taken away) that we speak of it as a "modern" state.

In distinguishing police from bank robbers in terms of the legitimacy the modern state gives to one but not to the other, we must be careful to specify exactly what kind of legitimacy the state can confer. Strictly speaking, the modern state confers only *legal* legitimacy and nothing more. That is, it says only that police have the legal right to use coercive force and bank robbers don't. It does not say that policing is moral and robbing banks is not, even though according to other sources of legitimacy this may be true. The state does not confer *moral* legitimacy.

This distinction between moral and legal legitimacy is important because throughout history, in many states (Nazi Germany, for instance) police enjoyed a legal legitimacy to do certain things that are morally outrageous. Likewise, it can be said of some criminal acts that although they are illegal (being illegal is, by definition, what makes them "criminal"), in certain situations they are morally defensible. A French Resistance fighter who robbed a Nazi bank to fund Resistance efforts would be a criminal, but most of us would applaud the morality of such a crime.

To get rid of the problem that the bank robber poses for our means-based definition of police we can say that in the modern state, police are

Institutions or individuals given the right to use coercive force by the state

Police and Prize Fighter, Football Players, Schoolteachers, Prison Guards, the Military, and Parents. We are making progress, but this modification of our definition still leaves us with the problem of distinguishing police from parents, the military, prize fighters, football players, schoolteachers, and prison guards. What is it about the police right to use coercive force that is different from the right to use it claimed by all of these others?

One major difference is *territorial*. It is obvious that this is so for football players, prize fighters, schoolteachers, and prison guards. They all enjoy their special right to use coercive force in limited areas. This is less obviously the case with the military. Nevertheless, we can say of the military that its principal job is to defend or extend by force the state's *external* boundaries. When the military is employed domestically, as is sometimes the case with the U.S. National Guard, we say that its been brought in to assume a "police" role. In other words, in such situations the military becomes a police.

Police and Parents. This territorial distinction still leaves us with the problem of distinguishing parents from police. Are parents police? Their rights to use coercive force are not territorially limited. They can spank their little brats on the streets, in shopping centers, and just about anywhere else they want to. The difference is that parents' rights to use coercive force is limited to their own children (or in special cases to children whom the state has placed in their care). The parent who tries to spank some other parent's child, no matter how much the little monster deserves it, risks both criminal and civil liability.

The parents' problem and the territorial problem in defining police can be handled by modifying our definition in two ways. First, we add the word "general" before the phrase "right to use coercive force." By "general" we mean that the police right to use coercive force is not limited to specific persons or specific locations. Second, we will tack on to the end of the definition the phrase "within the state's domestic territory." We do this to acknowledge that the territorial limits of police rights to use coercive force are the state's outer boundaries. Beyond those boundaries the use of coercive force is the province of the military.

With those two modifications in place our definition of police now reads:

> *Police are institutions or individuals given the general right to use coercive force by the state within the state's domestic territory.*

This definition of police solves all the problems that plague ends-based, norm-derivative definitions. It is true of all police everywhere and at all times. It excludes from our definition of police all sorts of institutions, activities, and individuals that do not belong there. And most important, this definition of police does not tell you anything about the hopes, fears, humor, history, or politics of its author. You do not know from this definition whether I am in any sentimental way for or against the police, nor do you know whether in any given case this definition refers to a good or bad, modern or ancient, corrupt or honest police. It is, as near as possible, a "value-neutral" definition.

These are obviously important achievements for a definition of police, and I have taken as much time as I have in showing you the development of this definition in the hope that you will appreciate them. But more important still, I have done so because defining police in this way encourages us to raise and explore a host of questions that norm-derivative definitions typically avoid, misunderstand, distort, or cover up. In fact, I am going to build the rest of this book upon the definition we have just constructed and the questions that it leads us to ask and try to answer.

The Idea of Police

So you will have some idea of what the above definition has got us into, let me list some of the very general questions we will take up in the rest of the book. Each of these questions raises lots of others and causes us to look at many old problems in a new way.

(1) Why do we have police at all? This question, which we shall take up in the remaining pages of this chapter, invites us to examine closely why in a modern democratic society we need to create a group of people with a general right to use coercive force. It encourages us to explore whether or not some other kind of group—one without the general right to use coercive force—could be created to do what police do. At the same time, it leads us to understand exactly what types of tasks the special competence of police—their general right to use coercive force—suits them to do.

(2) In modern democratic societies like the United States and England, why is most policing done by people who are in the direct and full-time employ of the state? What assurances

*do we have that a police organized in this way will not be
used as a weapon of political oppression by their employers?*
This question, which will form the basis for Chapters 2, 3,
and 4, will lead us into the history of police. Historical materials
are often dull and dusty and irrelevant to our contemporary
lives; by contrast, these chapters will be a history not of the
past but of the present. In Chapter 2 we will examine several
ways we have tried to get policework done without resorting
to a paid, professional police and why almost all of them have
been abandoned. In Chapter 3 we will look at how the politics
of policing shaped police agencies into the form that you and
I find them in today. And in Chapter 4 we will look at how
a mix of political and social forces shaped one very special
police role—the detective—into a cultural institution and a cultural
hero of gigantic proportions.

*(3) What is the relationship between police and the law?
How does the law limit what police do? How do police limit
what the law entitles them to do?* One of the duties we give
to police because they possess the general right to use coercive
force is the task of enforcing the law. In Chapter 5 we will
examine how they handle that responsibility, what special power
it gives them, what factors influence how they choose to exercise
it, and a variety of proposals to control the ways they use it.

(4) What makes a good police officer? What is good policing?
In Chapter 6 we shall take up the problem of what good policing
is and how we can create the kind of police officers and the
kind of police agencies in which good policing can develop
and flourish.

WHY DO WE HAVE POLICE?

Why should it be that in a modern democratic society the
state should create an institution with a general right to use
coercive force? What does a police make available in modern
democratic society that no other institution can adequately pro-

vide? These are questions that are almost never asked by those who start their study of police with a norm-derivative definition because their definition deludes them into thinking that they already know. These questions are crucial because any institution with the general right to use coercive force obviously is potentially dangerous. The American experience with police corruption, police brutality, and an unhappy history of all sorts of abuses of police power is evidence enough of this point. But we can add to it the even sadder experiences of other nations—the Soviet Union, Albania, Haiti, El Salvador, and Nicaragua, to name but a few. Surely, given such a history of corruption and abuse, both in the United States and elsewhere, any citizen of a democratic nation would be well advised to ask why it is that some less dangerous institution cannot be created to do what police do.

Our definition of police leads us to answer these crucial questions in a very special way—namely, to say that even in the most free and democratic of societies there are situations requiring the attention of someone with a general right to use coercive force. To appreciate why this is so, let's consider an example.

I share a property line with my neighbor. About one foot to my side of the property line there stands my horticultural pride and joy: a 25-foot apple tree. (Needless to say, a small portion of this gorgeous tree graces my neighbor's yard.) Though the tree is mine and I am willing to share its bounty with my neighbor, he does not like apples. He likes still less the fact that my apples fall off, rot, and litter his yard. One day he gets fed up with my stinking apples and yells to me that he is going to cut down my tree unless I do. "No way," I say. He revs up his chain saw.

Modern democratic society offers me two options in such a situation. First, I can drive to court and file a civil suit against my neighbor and, years hence, recover damages from him. The problem with this remedy is that I love my apple tree and don't want it cut down even if at some time in the future I am rewarded handsomely for its loss. Hence, modern democratic society offers me another option: call the cops and get them to stop my chain saw-wielding neighbor before his chain bites bark. What police have that suits them to this task is a right to use coercive force. That is, they can tell my neighbor to stop and if he doesn't, they can use whatever force is necessary to stop him.

This is not true of me, of course. I do not have a general right to use coercive force. Modern democratic society would look very dimly on me if I appeared on the scene with a gun and threatened to blast my neighbor and his revving chain saw into the great orchard in the sky.

"Something-ought-not-to-be-happening-about-which-something-ought-to-be-done-NOW!" The example above should not be understood to mean that the reason modern democratic societies must have police is to keep neighbors from killing one another in apple tree disputes. Rather, the example is offered as but one instance of a general type of situation that requires the attention of police, rather than some other agency or institution without a right to use coercive force.

Such situations have been defined by police sociologist Egon Bittner (1974:30) as situations in which "something-ought-not-to-be-happening-and-about-which-something-ought-to-be-done-NOW!" You will note that Bittner's definition has two parts to it, each of which you must understand precisely. The first part refers to "something-ought-not-to-be-happening" types of situations. Bittner could have merely said "illegal," but he did not for a very good reason. The police role is not restricted to attending to illegal acts. It is much broader than that. It may involve moving a crowd back from a fire scene so that fire fighters have room to work, removing disabled vehicles that are blocking traffic at an accident scene, turning off a gushing fire hydrant on a hot summer city street, calling on an elderly man who reports hearing suspicious noises outside his window at night, or a thousand other not necessarily illegal "ought-not-to-be-happening" types of situations to which police in modern democratic societies routinely attend.

The "about-which-something-ought-to-be-done-NOW" part of Bittner's definition is subtle and a bit more tricky to unravel.

The most critical word in Bittner's phrase is "now." It indicates that all of the "ought-not-to-be-happening" types of situations he describes in the first part of his definition have another distinctive feature: They cannot await a later resolution. I cannot wait until my apple tree is cut down any more than the fire fighter can wait for people to move, than traffic can wait for the owners of the wrecks to move them, or than the old man can wait to find out that the noise outside his window is actually an intruder. The crucial element is time.

What the general right to use coercive force gives to police is the right to do something *now*. It does so because despite resistance or protest by participants or observers in any about-which-something-ought-to-be-done-NOW situation, the general right to use coercive force gives police the right to overcome any and all opposition immediately. This, of course, does not mean that in every about-which-something-ought-to-be-done-NOW situation police actually use coercive force. Most people obey police orders and instructions without having to be physically coerced to do so. It only means that if we do not, the police have a legitimate right to make us do so *now*.

One final point about "something-that-ought-not-to-be-happening-and-about-which-something-ought-to-be-done-NOW!" situations. Bittner does not specify what the "something" is that the police ought to do situations of this type. Considering the mind-boggling variety of situations modern police are regularly called upon to handle, Bittner wisely leaves his "something" wholly undefined. You should not make the error of thinking that he means by it "arrest." In fact, according to the best research, the typical tour of duty for a police officer in the high-crime areas of three of the nation's largest cities (Boston, Washington, D.C., and Chicago) *does not involve the arrest of a single person.*[3]

In summary, then, to the question "Why is it that we have police?" we can say "We have them to deal with all those problems in which coercive force may have to be used." You will realize that this is a vastly different answer from anything a norm-derivative definition would have led us to say. But you should also note that although this answer is the most accurate way to describe the role of the police, it tells us nothing about who should play that role, why they should play it, or what can be done to shape, control, or influence the way it is played. These are the questions we shall begin to take up in Chapter 2.

DISCUSSION QUESTIONS

1. Look up the definition of "police" in whatever dictionary you have available. Is it a "norm-derivative" or "means-based" definition? If it is norm derivative, in what ways does it tell you about what the author of the definition hopes the police are or will be?

2. While you have your dictionary out, look up definitions of some other parts of the criminal justice system (law, court, corrections, prison, lawyer, judge, etc.). Are these definitions you find of them norm-derivative or means-based? Do they tell us what these parts or the criminal justice system are or do they reflect hopes for what they should be?

NOTES

1. This answer is Egon Bittner's and he has given it in slightly different ways in the two most important theoretical studies of police ever written: *The Functions of Police in Modern Society* (1980) and "Florence Nightingale in Pursuit of Willie Sutton: A Theory of Police" (1974). This chapter and the entire theoretical approach of this book is grounded on these two revolutionary works by Bittner.

I will also note that I have used "coercive force" instead of merely "force" to distinguish between the application of physical strength in interpersonal situation (e.g., getting a drunk into the back seat of a police car) and its application in a merely physical maneuver (e.g., prying the cap off a mustard jar).

2. The results of this study are to be found in Albert J. Reiss, Jr., *The Police and the Public* (1971). Although the research was conducted nearly 20 years ago (1966), its findings are still relevant and it remains the largest quantitative observational study of police to date.

2

VARIETIES OF
AVOCATIONAL POLICING

If about-which-something-ought-to-be-NOW! problems require the attention of someone with a general right to use coercive force, who should that someone be? Should it be the uniformed, armed, state-salaried, full-time, professional police of the kind you and I expect to arrive when we "call the cops"? Should it be specially designated private citizens, serving on a part-time, unpaid, voluntary basis? Or should we give the general right to use coercive force to everyone and thus remove the need for any special institution of police? Such questions probably seem strange to you. Since 1829, when the first modern police were introduced in London, and certainly since 1845, when New York City first placed an American version of a modern police on its streets, our imaginations of what a police can be have become progressively limited. To a modern American it seems almost perverse to ask whether or not we could get policing done without resorting to a modern, state-salaried, professional police. The fact is, however, that prior to 1829 in England and 1845 in the United States we did exactly that. We got the vast majority of policework done by calling upon private citizens to do it. Today, although private citizens can and do occasionally police, their policing responsibilities are minuscule. By and large, over the past century we have taken the right, obligation, and inducement to police away from private citizens and turned them over to full-time employees of the state.

In this chapter I want to do two things. First, I want to loosen up your imagination about what a police can be. I want to expose you to a wide variety of police systems that are

radically different from the kind of police we know today.
What makes them so different is that all of them are ways
of getting policework done by having private citizens do it,
not as a job but as an avocation—a part-time, often unpaid,
amateur activity. Second, I want to evaluate whether or not
any of these systems of avocational policing seems to provide
a reasonable and workable alternative to the full-time, state-
salaried, professional police we currently employ. If they do,
it is certainly in our interest as taxpayers to adopt them. If
they don't, their defects ought to show why we might have
a reason to expect that the professional police we pay for might
just serve us better.

OCCASIONAL AVOCATIONAL POLICING

In modern society we all engage in policing in some remote,
indirect, or occasional ways. For example, we retain the right
to police—that is, to use coercive force with the state's blessing—on
those occasions when we are forced to do so in self-defense.
The state is very careful about the way it grants this right
and often requires that no matter what the provocation, we
must exhaust all reasonable means of retreat before using coercive force to defend ourselves.[1] It can also be said that in
modern society we "police" when we "call the cops" to report
some form of "something-ought-not-to-be-happening-about-
which-something-ought-to-be-done-NOW!" situation. Of course,
we are not the ones who possess a general right to use coercive
force in such situations, but nevertheless, there is a remote
and indirect sense in which we police by mobilizing the state's
police on such occasions. Finally, there is an exceptionally remote
and indirect way we can be said to police when we attend
public meetings or vote for certain politicians to attempt to
influence police practices. For most people in modern society
their whole relation to policing is limited to these three rare,
remote, or indirect forms.

OBLIGATORY AVOCATIONAL POLICING

There are, however, other forms of police obligations that the modern state sometimes imposes on its citizens. In recent U.S. and English history, they have included the requirement that a citizen notify the police when he or she has knowledge that a serious crime has been committed as well as the obligation to come to the aid of a police officer who requests assistance in making an arrest or preventing the commission of a crime. Most recently, however, England and many states in the United States have done away with misprision of felony laws, laws making it a crime to fail to report a serious crime to police.[2] Moreover, most states also recognize that imposing the obligation on citizens to come to the aid of police officers is not without its risks. In Delaware, where I live, a citizen can be sent to jail for up to six months and fined as much as $500 for refusing to come to the aid of a police officer who requests assistance (De. Code, Title 11, sec. 1241). But it also provides that a person who comes to the aid of police officer but does so incompetently but reasonably shall be relieved of civil liability should he injure someone. (De. Code, Title 11, sec. 1242). What this law recognizes is that there is no reason to expect that an average citizen called upon in an emergency should know how to police competently. In periods prior to the formation of the modern, professional police, English and American law made a quite different assumption. Let's consider some large-scale examples of it.

The Posse

Perhaps the most familiar device of obligatory avocational policing in American history is the sheriff's posse. Every American who has seen a Western movie has some idea what a posse is. The James boys ride into town and rob the bank, some rustlers rustle somebody's herd, or someone does some other untoward deed the sheriff cannot handle. The sheriff or some other town official then rounds up a group of sturdy men to apprehend the culprit or bring the situation under control. In the typical Western movie the raising of a posse is carried on with great fanfare and enthusiasm. But it is important to remember that what makes the posse a form of *obligatory* avocational policing is that if the sheriff told you you were needed and you refused to saddle up, you could be thrown into the pokey for refusing.

There were many problems with the posse as a way of getting policework done. One of the most important was that the posse, as a system of police, required certain special material and social conditions for its survival. One of these conditions was a production or work environment that could be easily interrupted while workers were off fulfilling police obligations. The farming and ranching economies of the frontier West were, at least during most seasons, ideally suited to posse policing. The modern production line, business office, or bureaucracy obviously is not.

Also, the posse required that those who were deputized provide their own tools of policing. In the Old West this meant a horse, arms, and perhaps some provisions. In addition, the idea of the posse assumed that those who were called upon to serve in it would have some skills in using the tools they provided. It was not an unreasonable assumption in the Old West that the average person called upon for posse policing could ride a horse, shoot a gun, and follow a track or trail. Needless to say, it would be foolhardy to assume that the average citizen in modern society could provide the tools of modern policing or would be sufficiently skilled in their use. In fact, as we noted above, those modern laws that relieve citizens from civil liability when they are called upon to aid a police officer are testimony to exactly that.

Frankpledge

A very old form of obligatory avocational policing, *frankpledge,* was organized in the south and east of England after the Norman

Conquest (1066) and remained at least nominally in effect in those parts of England until late in the thirteenth century.[3] It is worth thinking about as a form of obligatory avocational policing not only because understanding it can loosen our imagination about what a police can be but also because no police system before or since placed such a complete police burden on every average citizen. If nothing else, the study of it helps us realize by comparison just how minor the average citizen's police obligations are today.

The frankpledge police system required that every male above the age of twelve form a group with nine of his neighbors called a *tything*. Each tything was sworn to apprehend and deliver to court any one of its members who committed a crime. Tythingmen, as they were called, were also required to hold suspects in custody while they were awaiting trial and to make regular appearances in court to present information on wrongdoing by members of their own or other tythings. One way to understand tything is to see it as a very special kind of promise that each adult male had to make to the state. By being in tything each man promised, in advance of any wrongdoing, that he had already assembled a nine-man police force to apprehend, incarcerate, and deliver him to court if he did. The effectiveness of the frankpledge system of police rested on very severe fines, which were imposed upon all members of a tything if the tything failed to perform its required duties. These fines, of course, are what made frankpledge an *obligatory* avocational police system.

Described in this simple way, the frankpledge system appears to possess a highly social and relatively apolitical quality. It was, after all, a system in which almost all policing was done by private citizens in the private sector, a system in which each man at maturity was required to assume a portion of the policing obligations of his community. On the face of it, it would be hard to imagine a more decentralized police, a police more removed from the direct control of the state.

Despite appearances, quite the opposite was true. All police systems must be understood in relation to the social and political environment in which they operate. Frankpledge was a police system invented by the conquering Norman monarchy as an instrument of central government control. Prior to the Norman Conquest policing and the administration of justice was almost totally under the control of local lords and nobles. Frankpledge sought to take that control out of local hands and place it into the hands of the king.

It did so in a number of ways. First, all the money collected from tything fines went into the king's treasury. Second, tythings were supervised not by local lords and nobles, but by the medieval sheriff, the king's man. Third, delinquent tything members were brought not to manoral courts of local jurisdiction but to central courts whose justices were the king's appointees. The fact that frankpledge policing was never organized in the north and west of England, territories less affected by the Norman Conquest, is an indicator of the ability of nobles in those areas to resist what they saw as the infringement of the king's sheriffs on local autonomy.

The extent to which frankpledge was an instrument of the central government was a major factor in its deterioration and demise. From late in the twelfth century to late in the thirteenth a series of kings ascended to the throne who were unable or unwilling to give frankpledge policing the central government support it needed. Richard I (1189-1199) was off crusading. He may have been "Lion-Hearted," but he was a lousy administrator. His successor, John I (1199-1216), had his regal powers severly limited when the nobility forced him to sign the Magna Carta. John's feeble successor, Henry III, ruled with utter incompetence for more than half a century (1216-1272). He was defeated in battle and imprisoned by his own nobles in 1264. Even his son sided against him. During Henry's reign the royal courts to which tything members were to deliver those among them who had committed crimes met only every seven years! What this meant was that if a tything captured one of its delinquent members, it would have to pay for his incarceration for years until the case went to trial. This lack of central government support placed tythings in "no-win" situations. If they failed to capture a criminal tything member, they would be fined and financially ruined. If they captured him and had to pay for his incarceration for years before he went to trial, they would be financially ruined as well. Under these impossible conditions the tything system of police deteriorated and eventually fell apart.

If the monarchy had been stronger, more efficient, and able to give frankpledge the administrative and judicial support it needed, could it have survived as an effective police? The answer is probably "no." For in addition to its lack of central government support, frankpledge suffered from a serious internal defect. As a system of police it had no way of policing people who were laterally mobile, who moved from place to place and town to town. Vagrants, wandering beggars, traveling peddlers, and other transients could not be brought into frankpledge. No tything would be willing to accept the responsibility for them. Frankpledge was a system of police that even under the best of conditions could work only in an extremely stable, local environment.

The Parish Constable System

What replaced frankpledge was the parish constable system. The transition was gradual. As frankpledge deteriorated early forms of the parish constable system grew to replace it. In 1285 the Statute of Winchester was enacted, and it is usually from that date that we mark the beginning of the parish constable system. But it is best to understand it not as creating the parish constable system but as gathering together the central elements of the various early forms in which that system already existed.

The Statute of Winchester provided that one man from each parish would serve a one-year term as parish constable on a rotating basis. He would not be paid for his work, and it is unknown if or from whom early parish constables recovered their expenses. Each parish constable was responsible for organizing a group of watchmen who would guard the gates of the town at night. Like the parish constable himself, these watchmen were unpaid and selected from the parish population. In the event of a serious disturbance the parish constable was authorized to press the entire parish into police service by raising what was called the "hue and cry." A call to arms similar to the raising of an American posse, hue and cry required all males in the parish upon hearing it to drop what they were doing and come instantly to the aid of the parish constable. The Statute of Winchester also required all citizens to keep arms in their homes so as to be able to support the parish constable with force when he asked them to do so. Finally, the parish constable was also required to perform the old frankpledge duty of delivering offenders to court as well as some newer duties, such as executing court orders for corporal punishments: maiming, whipping, burning with hot irons, and the like.

The Statute of Winchester provided for fines for those who refused to serve as parish constables when it came their turn to do so. But as you may now already appreciate, it would be a mistake to see the parish constable system as obliging only one man in each parish to police. It required, under threat of fine or other punishment, a variety of police services from every parish member. From the obligation to guard the gates of the town at night, to responding without hesitation to the hue and cry, to keeping arms in one's home, the parish constable system was actually a series of obligatory police systems one inside the other.

Politically, the parish constable system was a mix of victories and concessions for local government. It conceded, in a way frankpledge did not, that policing would be a local government responsibility. The constable was originally appointed by a manoral court of local jurisdiction. The fees and fines the parish constable collected went into local treasuries. In its early years the position of parish constable was a local office of considerable responsibility and distinction. However, as the office of parish constable evolved, a series of central government measures gradually made the work of the parish constable less dignified, more burdensome, and more subordinate to the political ambitions of the central state.

The process began in 1361 with passage of the Justices of the Peace Act. It established over the office of parish constable a layer of justices who were officials not of the parish but of *county* or *municipal* government. But unlike the office of parish constable, which was typically filled by shopkeepers, craftsmen, and other undistinguished townspeople, the office of justice of the peace was normally an appointment for wealthy gentlemen. This difference in status eventually transformed the parish constable from an officer of considerable importance in parish government to a rather lowly and amateur errand boy for county justices.

Between the fifteenth and eighteenth centuries the office of justice of the peace underwent a devastating transformation. The justice of the peace, like the parish constable, was unpaid. In the early years of the office this did not matter because the position was filled by persons of independent wealth who often saw service as justice of the peace to be a duty and opportunity appropriate to their high position in the community. Justices of the peace were appointed to their county or municipal offices by central government authorities. However, as conflicts arose between these county and municipal justices and the central government, the central government began to find it politically convenient to appoint as justices men who were less independent, less troublesome, and more sympathetic to central government ambitions. Often this meant denying appointment as justice to wealthy gentlemen and local lords and nobles, who had an interest in preserving local autonomy, and appointing in their place less distinguisded local men, many of whom could not afford to serve as justices for free.

What happened was that these justices began to charge stiff fees for their services. They had little choice but to do so, but the necessity of having to live off of the fees they collected for doing justice eventually led to corruption of the office. Merely being charged with an offense could bring financial ruin. As this corruption progressed, the office itself became disgraced. Not only did men of integrity and ability refuse to serve as justices, but men of almost openly corrupt ambitions sought it out. Finally, of course, the effects of the utter corruption of the office of justice of the peace trickled down upon the parish constable—the corrupt justice's errand boy.

To add to the parish constables' problem of the corruption of their superiors, their duties increased. As the feudal system broke down, the populations in towns and cities grew enormous-ly. The number of vagrants, beggars, and unlanded poor, who had little oportunity to earn a living except by theft, transformed the parish constable's job, theoretically a part-time, public ser-vice responsibility, into a full-time, year-long, unpaid vocation.

Although I have described the evolution of the office of parish constable in terms of a battle over local control of po-licing, it should not be viewed as some kind of simple conflict between the wishes of the king and Parliament and those of "the people." It is doubtful that anyone who actually had to do the work of parish constable cared much about anything but the fact that it had to be done, unpaid, by private hands. In the words of Beatrice and Sidney Webb, unquestionably the most thorough students of the history of the parish constable system:

> The little farmers or innkeepers, jobbing craftsmen or shopkeepers, who found themselves arbitrarily called upon to undertake ar-duous and complicated duties and financial responsibilities; ordered about during their year of service by justices of the peace; . . . at the beck and call of every inhabitant; losing time and money and sometimes reputation and health over their work; with no legal way of obtaining any remuneration for their toil and pains,— often felt themselves to be, not the rulers, but the beasts of burden of the parish [Webb and Webb, 1906].

In the eighteenth century the sentiments the Webbs describe encouraged a variety of practices that further deteriorated the parish constable system. One of the most common was for the person whose turn it was to serve as parish constable to hire a stand-in. Because the person who was hired would have to be paid for his year of service, the chief job qualification for a parish constable's stand-in soon became his willingness to work cheap. Typically, the men who were hired were too physically or mentally infirm to qualify for other work. Often the village idiot served as parish constable.

Another way of escaping service as a parish constable was to buy or earn what was called a "Tyburn Ticket."[4] This was a certificate issued to anyone who apprehended and prosecuted a felon to conviction. It exempted that person or anyone he sold it to from service as a parish constable. The Tyburn Ticket was, in effect, an eighteenth-century "get out of parish constable free" card. They sold commonly for £10 to £15 and in some cases for as much as £300. A century later, in 1829, £10 would have paid the salary of one of London's new "bobbies" for more than five weeks.

The deterioration and demise of the parish constable system illustrates the central flaw in all systems of obligatory avocational police. As the work becomes more difficult, demanding, or time-consuming, obligatory avocational policing takes on the characteristics of forced labor. Unpaid, it has to compete with earning a living. Motivated only by the threat of punishment, it becomes unwilling and resistant. Offering no one any reason to learn or cultivate the skills necessary to do it well, it becomes undependable, uneconomic, and of poor quality. In short, the more we expect a police to do, the less we can expect obligatory avocational police to do it. For all of these very good reasons, obligatory avocational systems cannot serve as a basis for a satisfactory modern police.

VOLUNTARY AVOCATIONAL POLICING

There is another way of getting policework done, a way that does not involve threatening people with punishment should they fail to do it. We will call it *voluntary avocational policing.* Voluntary avocational police police because they want to. Their motives are their own, and they are virtually unlimited. They can be racial or social justice as well as racial or social hatred. Motives can be community defense or persecution, heroic ambitions or frustration and despair. In the category of voluntary avocational police are vigilantes, lynch mobs, unpaid auxiliary police, and neighborhood and community watches and patrols. Because it raises so many of the issues central to understanding voluntary avocational policing, let's review vigilante policing in some detail.

The American Vigilante Tradition

American vigilante movements grew up in response to a typical American problem: the absence of effective law and order in frontier regions. In areas where law did not reach or where it was represented only by the efforts of a single sheriff or a sheriff and a few deputies, disorganized individual citizens were unable to defend themselves or their property against groups of criminals who could prey upon them with little fear of apprehension. Justifying their actions by appealing to a natural right of self-defense and self-preservation and pointing to the obvious impotence of official police, thousands of citizens of hundreds of frontier towns organized themselves into vigilante groups. They called themselves variously "regulators," "slickers," "committees of safety," "committees of vigilance," or merely "vigilantes."

In American history, at least 326 but possibly as many as 500 vigilante movements were organized between 1767 and 1900.[5] The first such movement, a group called "The Regulators," was formed in colonial South Carolina, but it is one of the very few vigilante groups to organize in an Eastern coastal state. Vigilantism spread in two great waves with the movement of the western frontier, first into the Mississippi Valley, Great Lakes, and Gulf Coast states and later onto the Great Plains, Rocky Mountains, and Pacific Coast. About a third (116) of the known vigilante groups were first-wave Eastern groups that disbanded by 1860. The other two-thirds (210) were second-wave Western groups, some of which continued to operate until the turn of the century. In terms of sheer numbers of vigilante movements, Texas led the way with 52, followed by California with 43.

Vigilante groups ranged in size from units with a dozen members to gigantic organizations, such as the San Francisco Vigilance Committee, with a membership of 6000 to 8000. The average movement included more than a hundred members. Most vigilante organizations had a constitution or a set of by-laws to which members swore allegiance. The typical vigilante group gave the outlaws they captured some version of a formal trial. Witnesses were sworn. The accused received counsel or an opportunity to defend himself. The crowd assembled at the trial or the vigilantes themselves formed the jury. Acquittals were rare. Some movements punished some of those they convicted by whipping or expulsion, but death by hanging, usually within hours of the verdict, was the most common sentence. The 326 vigilante groups of which there is record are known to have executed 729 people.

The membership of vigilante movements reflects the values and interests that vigilante actions were designed to preserve. In the leadership of most vigilante organizations were a town or a region's most powerful and prominent citizens: well-to-do businessmen; affluent farmers, planters, and ranchers; bankers, politicians, and eminent professional men. Two presidents (Andrew Jackson and Theodore Roosevelt), eight state governors (including Leland Stanford, Sr., founder of Stanford University), and four U.S. Senators had either been vigilantes or expressed strong support for vigilante movements. Although a local elite dominated the leadership of the typical vigilante group, the general membership was usually composed of middle-class men with a similar stake in preserving community peace, order, and property. Moreover, considering that most vigilante movements grew up in small towns or areas of fairly sparse population and that the average movement had somewhere between 100 and 300 members, many movements enjoyed broadscale community support.

Richard Maxwell Brown, the leading historian of the American vigilante tradition, suggests that most vigilante groups correspond to one of two models (1969: 143-145). There is the "socially constructive model" in which a vigilante group with broad-based community support overwhelmed outlaws and troublemakers and left the community in a more orderly and stable condition that it had been in before. By contrast, there is what Brown calls the "socially destructive model," describing that type of vigilantism that grew up without general community support, encountered resistance, and thrust a community into internal conflict and disorder. Such movements often ended in violent feuds between leaders of opposing vigilante groups or between pro-vigilantes and anti-vigilante forces.

Now that we know a little bit about what vigilantes are and have been in the United States, we can take up some problems in understanding them and what they have to teach us about voluntary avocational policing as a way of getting policework done. The first problem is whether or not it is proper to call vigilantes "police" at all. The fact is that they operated outside the law, illegally captured those they apprehended, and in capitally punishing those they found guilty committed the crime of premeditated murder. Is there any sense in which vigilante groups that regularly did so many profoundly illegal things could be seen as having been given the right to do so by the state?

The answer to this question depends entirely upon how one chooses to understand "the law." If "the law" is defined as what is written in state statute books, the answer to this question would have to be "no." In terms of what was written law, the state did not give vigilantes the right to use coercive force in the way they did. Sometimes, however, it is better to understand what "the law" is by examining how the state and its agents administer the written law in practice than it is to read what is written on the statute books. Although the written law prohibited what vigilantes did, by failing to provide an effective alternative and by failing to prosecute vigilante groups, the state gave them a kind of legal legitimacy. It was, of course, not the same kind of legitimacy it gave sheriffs, deputies, marshals, and other police the state openly legitimated. In effect, it said to vigilantes: "If you want to police, go ahead, the state will look the other way."

What we now know about the American vigilante tradition also helps us to understand why systems of voluntary avocational police are unacceptable in a modern democratic society. The problem with them is that they cannot be controlled. Voluntary avocational police do policework because they want to. Sometimes their motives are acceptable to most people in a particular community at a particular time, and the way they choose to express them leaves the community safer, more stable, and secure. At other times those motives lead voluntary avocational police to acts that leave communities in terror and near civil war. Because it is their own motives that drive voluntary avocational police to take up policework, it is extraordianrily difficult to control who and where and on whom they work or what they see fit to do.

The Tradition Continues. Although voluntary avocational systems of policing do not provide the type of control necessary to make them acceptable police systems in modern democratic society, this very lack of ability to control when they emerge and what they do should lead us to expect that they will not disappear. If people feel passionately that some problem requires attention by persons with a right to use coercive force and the state fails to provide those persons, the social soil is prepared for the growth of a voluntary avocational police movement.

In recent years situations of this type have given birth to groups as varied as the "Maccabees," a predominantly Hasidic Jewish radio-car patrol of some 250 residents of the Crown Heights area in Brooklyn, the "Deacons for Defense and Justice," an organization set up in a number of Southern states to protect marchers and civil rights activists; the "North Ward Citizens Committee," a force organized in an Italian area of Newark, to deter criminal activity and discourage predation and rioting by people from the nearby black Central Ward; and "Operation Interruption," an "armed police militia" of at least 200 core members formed in New York City's Harlem to conduct a "black fight against black crime."

But the best-known and largest organized group in the modern American vigilante tradition is the "Guardian Angels." Formed by Curtis Sliwa in New York City in early 1979, the organization grew to more than 700 members. Dressed in distinctive white tee-shirts and red berets, the streetwise young men and women of the Guardian Angels patrolled the streets and subways of New York City. Although they were unarmed, many were trained in martial arts. New York City residents soon learned to feel safer on a late-night subway train when a Guardian Angel was aboard.

By 1982 the Guardian Angel movement had spread to more than 40 cities across the country. But even though half a dozen of those cities gave them official recognition in the form of ID cards and special passes with which to ride the city's transit system free of charge while on patrol, most cities have refused to recognize or extend support to the Guardian Angels in any way. The specific reasons for official resistance are varied, but all of them stem from the difficulties of controlling a voluntary avocational police. Unable to control the selection, training, supervision, or discipline of those who become Guardian Angels, many cities fear that they would open themselves to civil liability were they to give official support to the Guardian Angels. Other cities fear that in some situations the Angels' presence might provoke rather than avert trouble, and still others believe that the answer to citizen's fears is not to encourage the development of amateur groups like the Guardian Angels but to strengthen the city's paid, professional police. In one particularly unfortunate instance in Newark, New Jersey, in 1982, a Guardian Angel was mistakenly killed by a police officer as the Angel was trying to come to the assistance of a citizen who was being mugged.

ENTREPRENEURIAL AVOCATIONAL POLICING

There is a fourth and final way to get policework done by private citizens on a part-time, amateur, avocational basis. It is to reward them on a per crime or per criminal basis for the policework they do. In this category, which we shall call entrepreneurial avocational policing, we find paid informants, bounty hunters, thief takers, and a host of unsavory others.

The Thief Takers

The largest experiment with entrepreneurial avocational policing in Western history began in England in 1962. It was in that year that the Highwaymen Act (4 & 5 William and Mary, c 6, 7, 8) was passed. It contained three provisions. First, it provided that anyone who captured and prosecuted a thief to conviction would be entitled to a £40 reward. (This amount would probably be a rough equivalent to the buying power of $2500 in 1985 U.S. dollars). Second, it provided that the person who captured the thief and prosecuted him to conviction would be entitled to keep the thief's horse, guns, money, and just about anything else he owned that was not stolen. Third and finally, the Highwaymen Act gave a Royal Pardon for his own crimes to anyone but a convicted felon who informed on at least two thieves and secured their convictions. The strategy of this last provision of the law was clear: By paying one felon to convict two, the state was getting a bargain.

Unfortunately, the law underestimated the ingenuity of those who took up its invitation to become entrepreneurial avocational police and the state got a great deal more than it had bargained for. A small army of mercenaries grew up in response to the provisions of the Highwaymen Act. Thief takers, as they were called, mixed bribery, extortion, blackmail, perjury, and murder in a vicious combination that served to increase crime rather than control it.[6]

The £40 reward was a decent sum, but it was not enough to justify risking one's life by confronting any of the large and well-armed gangs that roamed eighteenth-century London. Taking on such formidable opponents was particularly unwise when one could earn the same amount of money by false arrest and false testimony against a perfectly innocent citizen. Thief taking also offered opportunities for acting as an *agent provocateur*. By posing as a friend or a seasoned criminal, a thief taker could encourage a child or an unwary novice to commit a crime or become an accessory to one and then turn around and take him for it. Thief taking also encouraged the practice of acting as a receiver of stolen goods, in that thief takers would permit thieves to continue to steal as long as they sold their booty at bargain rates to thief takers. Finally, when a thief taker apprehended a felon who could be expected to pay more in blackmail fees than the £40 his conviction would be worth to the thief taker, it was in the thief taker's economic interest to let him go. In a particularly ingenious manipulation of all of these corrupt possibilities the Highwaymen Act made possible, one very famous thief taker, Jonathan Wild (1682-1725), built what might well have been the largest organized criminal corporation in British history.[7]

The thief taker system, despite the fact that thief takers grew to be among the most despised elements in English society, continued to expand. In the years between the Highwayman Act of 1692 and the Metropolitan Police Act of 1829, which created London's first professional police, many crimes other than theft were added to the list for which thief takers could collect their £40 rewards. In many cases private individuals, companies, and prosecution societies added rewards of their own to the £40 the state offered.[8]

The thief taker system may be seen as an attempt to reverse the motivational strategy of obligatory avocational policing. In doing so it created a very active work, not unlike voluntary avocational policing in its intensity. But the problem with the thief taker system—and, indeed, with all systems of entrepreneurial avocational police—is that the ideal of greed is too narrow a motive on which to base a satisfactory system of police. There is nothing wrong, of course, with using an offer of money to get people to do policework, or any kind of work for that matter. But if that motive is all there is to induce people to do the work and control the way it is done, people will quickly find ways to corrupt the purposes they serve. By rewarding entrepreneurial avocational police on a piece-rate basis criminals were produced, but not those that were the targets of the Highwayman Act or subsequent legislation that expanded it to include other felons. The criminals created were the thief takers themselves, and the felons they delivered to court were often criminals they had manufactured to sell to the state at £40 per head.

The Bounty Hunter

In one way at least the American bounty hunter system, the nearest equivalent to the English thief takers, may be regarded as something of an improvement. It added a single measure of control that its English ancestor never had: It generally specified *who* rather than what category of felon the bounty hunter could take.[9] Thus it closed off the opportunity to make criminals to fit a crime. But neither system of entrepreneurial avocational police could control who would do policework or how (anywhere between "Dead or Alive" as the old bounty poster read) it would be done.

CONCLUSIONS

Having said this much about the various forms of avocational policing, we may now move on to the next chapter, where we will take up the modern police vocation. But first let us review what we have learned by looking at avocational policing and see how it helps us to approach the next topic on our agenda.

The first point is that no police system can be understood apart from the social and political system in which it works. We saw this to be true of all the avocational police systems we looked at in this chapter, and we should expect to find it true of the professional police systems we examine in the next.

Second, we have established that policing is work. Like most work it requires effort, energy, a certain level of competence, and motives to get it done. Also, like most work it can be done under many different working arrangements, some of which, obviously, are more desirable than others. But unlike most work, policing can be done not only too passively but too aggressively as well. In addition, policing provides opportunities for abuse and corruption that far exceed those in most other occupations.

Third, the institutional history of having policework done by anyone who felt a need to do it (voluntary avocational policing), by coercing people to do it (obligatory avocational policing), or by offering rewards to people to do it (entrepreneurial avocational policing) is a history of severe problems. Modern democratic society rightly discourages these ways of getting policework done. Standing alone, none of these forms seems to provide the type of stability, reliability, or basis for the social control of policing that is necessary in modern society.

If all of this is so, then we may now ask the critical question that will lead us through the next chapter. Why should we be able to control a state-salaried, professional police any better than the avocational police systems we have just considered? Put differently, when policing is made a full-time vocation, when it becomes a job, what single means of controlling it becomes possible that was not possible under any of its avocational forms? You will find the answer to this question on the first page of the next chapter, but before looking there, see if you can figure it out for yourself.

DISCUSSION QUESTIONS

In this chapter we have looked at a wide variety of forms of avocational policing, ways of getting policework done by having private citizens in the private sector do it as an avocation rather than a job. There is another very interesting way in which we might get policework done without resorting to a police that was in the direct employ of the state. It would be to let private industries go into the police business with full police powers. Under such a system a town or city or county or state would contract with a private company for police services. Do you consider this a reasonable alternative to a state-salaried police? Is it a way we might get policing done cheaper and more efficiently than we do now? Would such a police be more or less dangerous politically than a state-salaried police?

NOTES

1. The Model Penal Code of the American Law Institute (s. 3.04 of Tentative Draft No. 8) endorses what has been called the "retreat to the wall" doctrine:

> The use of deadly force is not justifiable . . . if the actor knows . . . that he can avoid the necessity of using such force with complete safety by retreating or by surrendering possession of a thing to a person asserting a claim of right thereto or by complying with a demand that he abstain from any action which he has no duty to take, except that:
>
> (1) the actor is not obliged to retreat from his dwelling or place of work, unless he was the initial aggressor.

A number of states, by contrast, follow what is called the "true man" rule, which provides that a person may stand his ground and meet force with force. But even in such jurisdictions (inspired by an image of how John Wayne would behave when confronted with a threat of force), if the person threatened acts in such a way to bring on the difficulty, he must either retreat or face a charge of, at minimum, manslaughter, if he uses deadly force. (Ol' Duke never started fights, he just finished them.) It might be worth your while to find out where your state stands on this question.

2. The U.S. Code (18 U.S.C.A., s.4) contains a misprision of felony provision, but it requries an affirmative act of concealment, making it more of a conspiracy law than a misprision of felony law. Most states take the position that the misprision of felony obligation is too severe (see Holland v. State, Fla. App. Ct., 1974, 302 So. 2d 806) and replace it with an obligation of either not compounding a felony or not hindering prosecution.

3. The materials in this section are taken from William Alfred Morris's classic study, The Frankpledge System (1910).

4. "Tyburn Tickets" earned their name from Tyburn Hill, the place in London where most criminals were brought for execution (not far from Hyde Park's famed Speaker's Corner and near London's Playboy Club). They were created in 1699 by 10 William III c.12 and not repealed until 1827 by 7 and 8 George IV c.27.

5. All materials on the American vigilante tradition are drawn from the works of Richard Maxwell Brown (1969, 1975).

6. On the thief takers see Patrick Pringle (1958, 1965).

7. The definitive study of Jonathan Wild is Gerald Howson's *Thief-Taker General, The Rise and Fall of Jonathan Wild* (1970). See also Klockars (1980) for a study of the career of Wild that shows how it cautions us about the dangers of some contemporary police methods.

8. A detailed description of these private prosecution societies and associations may be found in Leon Radzinowicz's *History of The English Criminal Law* (1948, 1957). See especially Vol. II, *The Enforcement of the Law*.

9. One notable exception to this rule is the case of what John Hope Franklin has called "quasi-free negroes" (1969). Slaves who had legitimately earned their freedom in the South were in constant danger of being kidnapped by bounty hunters, having their certificates of freedom destroyed, and being returned elsewhere to slavery.

3

SHAPING THE POLICE VOCATION: PATROL

When policing is made a full-time, paid vocation, when it becomes a job, what special and powerful means of controlling it becomes possible that was not possible under any of its older avocational forms?

The answer is that only when policing becomes a full-time, paid occupation does it become possible to dismiss, to *fire,* any particular person who makes a living doing it. The state could only hire thief takers, bounty hunters, and paid informants; it could not fire them. At best (or worst) it turned the other way when vigilantes did their thing. Many modern cities would like nothing better than to be able to give Curtis Sliwa and his Guardian Angels the boot. Tythingmen and parish constables would have begged to be sacked. Because the option to take police officers' jobs away from them is the only essential means of controlling policework that separates the police vocation from all avocational arrangements for doing it, how that option is used, by whom, and for what purposes are the cutting questions that will lead us toward understanding what any police vocation eventually becomes.

COPS AND BOBBIES

In this chapter we use those cutting questions to dissect major developments in the historical evolution of the modern English and American police. Both police systems share a common legal tradition, and the English police served as an explicit model for police systems in many American cities. The fact is, however, that from the very first days of their organization

American and English police were very different institutions. There is simply no comparison between the levels of brutality and corruption that have characterized the police of most American cities and London's "bobbies." Moreover, the attitude of the English citizenry toward its police has differed markedly from that of Americans toward theirs. For decades English surveys have shown that the English place a higher level of trust in bobbies than in any other occupational group.[1] By contrast, for much of American history we have regarded our police with contempt. It is only fairly recently in American history that policing has come to be regarded as something more than a dumping ground for men or women who could not find a "decent" job.

The basis for these and other dramatic differences between English and American police was established long ago. In 1829, when the Metropolitan Police Act made possible the formation of what the English called the "New Police," some 3000 men were needed to fill the new ranks. The entrance qualifications were minimal: Candidates had to be at least 5′11″ tall, under age 35, literate, reasonably healthy, and of good character. So that recruits would be familiar with the people they policed, Home Secretary Robert Peel and his first police commissioners, Col. Charles Rowan and Irish barrister Richard Mayne, agreed that they would seek those "who had not the rank, habits, or station of gentlemen" (Gash, 1961:502). The pay of the new constables, just over four shillings a day, assured that few gentlemen would apply. "From the start," says British police historian T. A. Critchley, "the police was to be a homogeneous and democratic body in tune with the people, and drawing itself from the people" (1967:52).

A similar sentiment for a "people's police" marked early U.S. police history. In 1844, the New York bill establishing the first modern police force in America ensured that all policemen would come from the wards in which they would serve. They were appointed to their posts by the mayor of New York "upon the nomination of the alderman, assistant alderman, and the two tax assessors of each ward. The mayor could reject or accept nominations and in cases of rejection new names would be submitted in the same manner as the original ones. In such a system, the real power lay with the alderman and assistant alderman of each ward" (Richardson, 1970:45-46). In other American cities similar arrangements served to tie policing to the lowest levels of local, municipal government.

It is precisely because the American police were local and tied to ward-level city government that Irish, Italian, and Jewish minorities were able to join police forces in the face of exclusion from other private and public sector occupations.[2] The ward leader knew that appointing minority men to police positions was not only a way to curry support of the ethnic vote but also a way to have on the police force in his own ward officers who owed their jobs to him. In recent American police history, this local political base of most police departments is one reason why significant numbers of black and Hispanic minorities made inroads into policing in advance of similar achievements in private industry.[3] So, despite the fact that the English are often inclined to attribute the success of their police to the popular origins of their constables, that alone cannot be responsible for this success. Throughout their history American police have been every bit as much of a "people's police" as the English.

The real difference lies not in popular representation or local control but in the way in which the English police administrators were able to employ the sheer technical power of administration. That power was directly grounded upon the ability to fire policemen who did not perform up to standard. No other difference between early American and early English policing is so dramatic or so important to understanding how those organizations evolved in such different ways.

Between 1830 and 1838 to hold the ranks of the New Police of London at a level of approximately 3300 men required nearly 5000 dismissals and more than 6000 resignations, most of the latter not being altogether voluntary (Lee, 1971:240). Although many bobbies quit the force because the pay was so low, in the first eight years of the existence of London's New Police, it is reasonable to estimate that *every position on the entire force was fired or forced to resign nearly three times over!* If that is not using the option to dismiss with a passion, it is hard to imagine what is.

By contrast, what turnover there was in early American police departments was heavily attributable to changes in local political elections. When a local ward leader or alderman got dumped, the patronage police he appointed got dumped too. In early American policing the option to fire was not so much an administrative tool as it was a consequence of political misfortune. In New York, for example, the first chief of police could not dismiss officers under his command. The tenure of the chief was limited to one year. Consequently, any early New York cop who was solidly supported by his alderman and assistant alderman could disobey a police superior with virtual impunity. So while the British were firing bobbies left and right for things like showing up late to work, wearing disorderly uniforms, and behaving discourteously to citizens, American police were assaulting superior officers, refusing to go on patrol, extorting money from prisoners, and releasing prisoners from the custody of other officers. For 12 years, despite regulations that required them to do so, the early New York policemen successfully refused to wear uniforms. In 1856 a compromise was reached by allowing officers in each ward to decide on the style and color it liked best. Imagine yourself the first chief of "New York's Finest" trying to control the police under your command but without the power to dismiss anyone who disobeyed your orders.

Perhaps the only good thing about the corrupt, inefficient, ineffective, and disobedient early American police is that as an institution it could not be well controlled by anyone—not even the local politicians. This is not to say that they could not call upon police thugs to disrupt voting, shield ballot box stuffing, and protect the criminal constituents who contributed to their campaigns. It simply means that the level of disorganization and incompetence was so high in early American police agencies that the use of police as a weapon of political control was limited to rather crude operations. Politically, the problem of most early American police agencies was trying to control and manage that agency while every day-to-day administrative decision could be overruled by any local politician.

By contrast, the English faced an altogether different type of political problem. For nearly a century prior to the formation of their New Police, the English had refused to create a full-time, state-paid police for fear that it would be used as a weapon of political control by the administrative branch of government. It was this fear that caused them to hang on so long to the obviously ineffective parish constable system and the corrupt and despised thief takers. The New Police, made obedient and disciplined by the sanction of dismissal, gave to the administrative branch of government precisely the kind of organization that could be used as an instrument of political oppression. In the face of this fear the political problem of the administrators of the New Police—Peel, Rowan, and Mayne—was to demonstrate that the New Police would be, as near as possible, politically neutral.

UNARMED, UNIFORMED, AND CONFINED TO PREVENTIVE PATROL

To this end Peel, Rowan, and Mayne imposed three major restraints on the New Police: (1) They would be *unarmed,* except for a small truncheon concealed beneath their coats; (2) they would be *uniformed;* and (3) they would be confined to *patrol* for the *prevention* of crime. Let's look at each of these restraints and the different political meanings each took on in England and the United States.

UNARMED

Politically, the main virtue of an unarmed police is that their strength can be gauged as the rough equivalent of their numbers. The political advantage of arms is that they can serve as multipliers of strength and increase the coercive capacity of an individual to levels that are incalculable. One man with a rifle can dominate dozens of unarmed citizens, with a machine gun hundreds, with a nuclear missile entire nations. One man with a stick is only slightly stronger than most others, and that difference can be quickly eliminated by picking up a sturdy bottle, baseball bat, rake, stone, hammer, or any other multiplier of individual strength that lies within reach. In 1829, the individual strength of their 3000-man, unarmed police force offered little to fear to London's 1.3 million citizens.

The second political virtue of an unarmed police, the style of policing it requires, in the long run is far more important to the politics of policing than any calculus of strength. Strength, because it is a property of individuals, can be attacked the moment the individual grows weary or becomes distracted. A single rifleman, machine gunner, or nuclear terrorist can hold large numbers of people at bay, but he is in big trouble the moment he falls asleep. Policing is, by definition, coercive. It must, at least on occasion, compel compliance from people who would like to do otherwise. But it cannot survive for long if every confrontation with citizens requires the actual use of coercive force.

How can police gain compliance from the people they police without resorting to the use of coercive force? Sociologically, at least three other bases for control are possible: *authority, power,* and *persuasion.* To understand how the British and American police shaped up into such very different institutions, it is important to understand the major differences between these bases for control of one person by another.

Authority. Of the four bases for control—authority, power, persuasion, and force—authority is the most powerful, the most social, and the most stable. It is marked by "unquestioning recognition by those who are asked to obey; neither coercion nor persuasion is needed" (Arendt, 1973:116). Those who obey authoritative commands do so without question because they understand those commands as right and necessary; right because the person or institution issuing the command is entitled to do so and necessary because a genuinely authoritative command precludes serious consideration of alternatives. To wait patiently for a red light to turn green before proceeding, even late at night when the way is obviously clear and there is no possibility of detection, is to evidence an authoritative relationship to the institutions of traffic control. In short, an authoritative red light means *Stop!* and that's that.

Power. Power, as distinct from authority, refers to "the chance of a man or a number of men to realize their own will in a communal action, even against the resistance of others who are participating in the action" (Weber, 1948:180). Understood in this way, power shares at least one important characteristic with authority and is distinguished profoundly from it by two others. The common feature is that both are *social* as opposed to individual forms of control. They both depend upon persons acting in concert, sharing and coordinating meanings and actions. If a citizen complies with a police officer's order out of deference to police power, what is obeyed is not merely the officer's command but the officer, the other officers who will follow, and the social, legal, economic, and political resources that will be brought to bear should the command be disobeyed.

Distinguishing power from authority are its relationship to *resistance* and *probability*. Unlike authority whose hallmark is unquestioning acceptance, power admits the contemplation and the calculation of the costs of resistance. Power is potential. It is a matter of the probability that *if* one resists one will be overcome. Persons who respond to a police command out of respect to power do so because they believe that resistance is not worth the gamble.

Persuasion. Like power, persuasion acknowledges resistance, but it goes one step further. It does not leave resistance potential but actively engages it with signs, symbols, words, threats, and arguments designed to overcome it. The arguments may be true or false, the threats real or hollow, the words harsh or soothing. But always their purpose is to create in the mind of the person being persuaded the belief that he or she ought to comply. We do not say of persons that they have been "persuaded" to do something until they come to believe they ought to do it.

Although persuasion is very much a part of policework, certain features of the situations police routinely encounter limit the opportunities for its use. One such important limitation is time. "About-which-something-ought-to-be-done-NOW!"

situations often require quick compliance with police orders. They simply do not permit police the leisure to do extensive persuasion. Also, in about-which-something-ought-to-be-done-NOW! encounters with citizens who do not have full control of their mental faculties (e.g., the high, the drunk, the hopeless, the obsessed, the scared to death, and the madder than hell), the task of persuading is extremely difficult. How does one communicate even the simple threat—"Do what I say or I will make you do it!"—to someone so irrational or delirious that they cannot even comprehend it?

How do these distinctions between the four bases upon which control can be established allow us to understand better the long-run consequences of the English decision to keep its police unarmed? What Peel and Rowan and Mayne knew was that unarmed, the New Police would not be able to control the situations they would have to deal with if their interventions were based upon individual officers' capacities to use coercive force. Without the benefit of multipliers of individual strength, too often they would be overcome by individuals who were stronger. Moreover, because they were unarmed, their threats to use coercive force would be unpersuasive. Instead, the early architects of the New Police attempted to create a police whose basis for taking control of situations was its authority and power. Unquestioned respect for the legitimacy of the constables was to be combined with the perception that they represented an institution of formidable capacities. Nowhere can this aspiration be seen more clearly than in the instructions Peel gave to his New Police constables about how they should conduct themselves while on patrol:

He [the constable] will be civil and obliging to all people of every rank and class.

He must be particularly cautious not to interfere idly or unnecessarily in order to make a display of his authority; when required to act he will do so with decision and boldness; on all occasions he may expect to receive the fullest support in the proper exercise of his authority. He must also remember that there is no qualification so indispensable to a police-officer as a perfect command of temper, never suffering himself to be moved in the slightest degree by any language or threats that may be used; if he does his duty in a quiet and determined manner, such conduct will probably excite the well-disposed of the bystanders to assist him, if he requires them [quoted in Critchley, 1967:52-53].

Peel's orders, which remain binding on bobbies to this day, clearly emphasize the extent to which the New Police constables were expected to develop a citizen respect for their authority that would, in turn, make it possible for them to do their work. There is even in Peel's first orders something of a threat to those constables whose conduct failed to create that respect. If they failed, there may be no well-disposed bystanders to come to their assistance when they require help.

Although each constable had a role in creating the respect for authority that is necessary for an unarmed police, it would be wrong to understand that authority to be owed to or based upon personal respect for individual constables. What Peel, Rowan, and Mayne wanted—and got, to a great degree because they used their power to fire any individual constable who did not work to help create it—was an authority owed equally to all constables because it was owed not to any individual officer but to the single, uniform temperament, code of conduct, style of work, and standard of behavior that every constable was expected to maintain.

In New York, Boston, and other American cities the modern police began, in imitation of London's bobbies, as unarmed forces.[4] In fact, in the earliest years of both the New York and Boston departments officers who carried guns against orders were often looked upon as cowards or wimps by both police administrators and fellow officers. A "real" policeman ought to have the muscle and the courage to handle himself on the street without resort to a concealed handgun. Their conduct on the streets quickly earned the early American police a reputation for being tough; but undisciplined, disobedient, and corrupt, they could not inspire respect for either their authority or their power. The problem, though, with trying to establish control based upon a reputation for toughness is that someone armed with a multiplier of strength can always prove to be tougher.

Both New York and Boston police learned this lesson the hard way—by having officers shot and stabbed or beaten by groups or individuals who did not hestitate to use weapons in confrontations with police. Gradually, officers in both departments began to arm themselves, concealing underneath their uniforms a variety of weapons they had purchased on their own or confiscated from prisoners. Although regulations prohibited it, superior officers began to condone the practice. By the late 1850s in New York and by the mid-1860s in Boston, the American police had, against orders, armed themselves. In an effort to control the type of weapons their officers carried, both departments eventually began issuing standard service revolvers.

The long-run effect of arming the American police can be understood only by appreciating how it shaped American police officers' sense of the source of their capacity to control the citizens with whom they dealt. While the London bobbies drew their capacity for control from the profoundly social authority and power of the institution of which they were a part, American cops understood their capacities for control to spring from their own personal, individual strength, multiplied if necessary by the weapons they carried on their hips. This understanding of the source of their capacity for control as their individual strength led American officers to see the work they did and the choices they made in doing it to be matters of their own individual discretion. Thus the truly long-run effect of the arming of the American police has been to drive discretionary decision-making to the lowest and least public levels of American police agencies. To this day, how an American police officer handles a drunk, a crazy, a belligerent motorist, a family argument, or a teenager with a joint of marijuana or a knife in his pocket is largely a reflection of that particular American police officer's *personal* style.

UNIFORMED

Politically, the requirement that police be uniformed is a guarantee that they will not be used as spies, that they will be given information only when their identity as police is known, and that those who give them information—at least when they do so in person—are likely to be noticed as they do so. The uniform also has the political advantage of increasing the possibility that the state can be held responsible for the acts that its own agents undertake, under orders or on their own initiative.

The Popay Incident. How strongly the English appreciated the importance of the uniform as a control on the political uses of their New Police can be seen from their reaction to the first known occasion on which a police constable broke the uniform's restraint. In 1833, a police sergeant named Popay infiltrated the National Political Union, a radical political organization opposed to both the prevailing government and the New Police. To accomplish his infiltration Popay disguised himself as a struggling artist and spent four months in his undercover role.

Popay became an active member of the National Political Union. He contributed money to the organization and spoke frequently at its meetings. In his speeches he urged members to go to extreme lengths to bring down the government and oppose the New Police. Undercover, Popay played one of the most contemptible of police roles, *agent provocateur*—one who provokes people to commit crimes so they can be arrested when they do.

Popay's charade came to an end when he was seen sitting in uniform in a police station by one of the other members of the National Political Union. The press was given the story and for weeks railed against the government and their band of spies, the New Police. In those weeks the New Police came very close to being abolished.

The police account of the Popay incident claimed that Popay had undertaken his *agent provocateur* role on his own initiative and fired him for doing so. But their version of the incident is hard to swallow. How the tight administration of the New Police could have overlooked the ununiformed undercover activities of one of its own sergeants for four months is a great mystery. Even more mysterious is where Popay got the money he gave to the National Political Union. It is probably the case that the Popay incident was not only the first occasion on which the New Police were discovered using constables as political spies but the first cover-up in New Police history as well. In the following year, 1834, the National Political Union held a large rally in London, which the New Police were assigned to control. At the rally the crowd got out of hand; three New Police constables were stabbed and one of the three died immediately. At the coroner's inquest the jury found, despite all evidence to the contrary, that the persons who had stabbed the constables had committed "justifiable homicide." The verdict was eventually quashed, but it made very clear to the New Police just how outraged the English people were at the actions of Popay and how determined they were to keep their New Police in uniform where they could be watched and held accountable for what they did.

The American sense of the politics of being uniformed was altogether different from the English. The law establishing the New York City police explicitly rejected the idea that they should be uniformed. The uniform, it was thought, would set the police apart from the people and create an undemocratic impression of police superiority. Ironically, however, when early New York police administrators imposed regulations requiring officers to wear uniforms, the officers who refused to wear them opposed them on exactly the opposite grounds. They saw uniforms not as a mark of undemocratic superiority but as a degrading subservience and inferiority that was incompatible with American democratic society's belief in equality.

Whatever political meaning was the more important basis for the early American police resistance to control of the uniform, the fact is that the modern American police uniform makes a different impression than the uniform the early police resisted in the mid-nineteenth century or the uniform the English bobby sports today. The modern English police constable's truncheon remains hidden beneath his blue coat, but the modern American police uniform is festooned with the forceful tools of the police trade. The gun, ammunition, nightstick, blackjack, handcuffs, and mace, all tightly holstered in shiny black leather and set off with chromium buckles, snaps, badges, stars, flags, and insignia suggest a decidedly military bearing. The impression intended is clearly not the restraint of the state but of the capacity of its domestic forces to overcome the resistance of even the most fearsome enemies.

The Military Analogy. To understand the politics of the military appearance of the American police uniform, it is necessary to see it as a reflection of a major reform movement in the history of the American police.[5] Beginning around 1890, American police administrators began to speak about the agencies they administered as if they were domestic armies engaged in a war on crime. The analogy, as with all great strokes of political rhetoric, was powerful and simple. It drew upon three compelling sources for its inspiration, and each of those sources had a direct policy implication.

First, the military analogy sought to connect the police with the victories and heroes of the military rather than the corruption and incompetence of local municipal politics. Understood in this way, the military analogy was a way of speaking about police that would help to create a respect for them that would make them and their work a more honorable profession.

Second, the military analogy played upon a sense of urgency and emergency. "There is a war going on in the streets of this country!" it cried, and unless police are given the manpower and resources they need to win the war on crime, the criminals will take over. This aspect of the military analogy is nearly as useful today as it was three quarters of a century ago in getting municipal governments and taxpayers to part with money for police salaries and equipment.

Third, and most important, the military analogy had as a crucial part of its reform agenda creating a relationship between police chiefs and politicians at the local level that was similar to the relationship between military generals and politicians at the national level. At the level of national politics Americans have always conceded that the question of whether or not to fight a war or expand it into a new area was a political decision. But at the same time we have also left the day-to-day conduct of battles and discipline of troops to military commanders. What the early chiefs wanted was the same kind of relationship with local politicians. There would be no question about the politicians' right to decide if and when and where the war on crime should be fought, but the conduct of the actual battles and the day-to-day discipline of the troops would be the chiefs' decisions. By getting the public and politicians to take the military analogy seriously, the early chiefs had found a way to wrest from the hands of politicians the tool they needed to discipline their troops: the option to fire disobedient officers. The uniform of the modern, war-ready American police officer is evidence of the early chiefs' victories in defining the American police as crime fighters. But the war on crime rhetoric that the early chiefs promoted to secure some essential reforms brought with it a host of problems that plague American police organizations to this day.

A major problem is the very idea of a war on crime. It is a war police not only cannot win but cannot, in any real sense, fight. They cannot win it because it is simply not within their power to change those things—such as unemployment, the age distribution of the population, moral education, freedom, civil liberties, ambition and the social and economic opportunities to realize it—that influence the amount and type of crime in any society. Moreover, any kind of real "war on crime" is something no democratic society would be prepared to let its police fight. We would simply be unwilling to tolerate the kind of abuses to the civil liberties of innocent citizens—to us—that fighting any kind of a "war" on crime would inevitably involve.

The fact that American police continue to advertise the reason for their existence as their role in fighting crime creates major problems for both police administrators and line officers. Police administrators continue to claim credit for decreases in the crime rate and take the blame for increases that are not their fault. Out of political necessity they routinely oversell the capacity of new equipment or larger numbers of officers to make the streets safer while they know—or at least should know—that it probably won't make any difference.

What patrol officers know is that while their chief is advertising the department's role in fighting crime, very little of what they do day in and day out has much impact on it. Consider that *the patrol officer's modal tour of duty does not involve* an arrest of any person (Reiss, 1971:19); that about half the calls to police involve requests for help with personal or interpersonal problems (Cumming et al., 1965); that the typical uniformed patrol officer in New York City makes about three felony arrests *per year* (National Commission on Productivitity, 1973, quoted in Bittner, 1974:25); that an individual patrol officer in Los Angeles can expect to detect a burglary no more than once every three months and a robbery no more than once every 14 *years* (Institute for Defense Analysis, 1967:12); that 83% of all the incidents handled by the Chicago police in one 28-day period of study were of a noncriminal nature (Reiss, 1971:75); and that the largest and most systematic study of patrol effectiveness ever done, the Kansas City Patrol Experiment, showed no difference in the amount of crime reported, the amount of crime as measured by community surveys, or the amount of citizen fear of crime when the level of random police patrol was eliminated, kept the same, doubled, or tripled (Kelling et al., 1974). We have no study to show that foot patrol reduces crime (Police Foundation, 1981) or that the speed at which police respond to reports of serious crime makes anything but the most minuscule difference in overall rates of apprehension of criminals (Spelman and Brown, 1983:160-166).

For patrol officers, the problems of policing in the name of crime while most of what they are called upon to do is not crime fighting are enormous. If they understand "real policework" to be fighting crime, they may soon come to see most of what they do as "bullshit" or mere "PR" (public relations) and come to resent it. In most departments, despite the fact that they will spend most of their time doing that kind of noncriminal work, it is unlikely that police will be trained to do it or that they will be recognized for doing that kind of work well. It is not uncommon for patrol officers to come to see their employers as hypocritical promoters of a crime-fighting image far removed from what they know to be the reality of everyday policework. They may seek to explain what they know to be their failure to do much about crime in terms of the lack of courage of their chief, the incompetence of the police administration, or of sinister political forces seeking to "handcuff" the police. If they do they are likely to wind up closing off what they regard as the disappointing reality of what they do in cynicism, secrecy, and silence—what has come to be called the occupational culture of policing. The patrol officers who come to think this way about their work and themselves may well work for a cowardly chief, probably suffer under incompetent administration, and are certainly constrained by the rights of others to their civil liberties. But they come to think this way less because they are burdened by these real problems than because they are victimized by their own profound misconception of what they are supposed to do—the false belief police chiefs began to promote three quarters of century ago that police could fight and win a war on crime.

The last of the spoils of the early chiefs' victories in their well-intended war on crime is the military administrative structure itself. Once considered to be a model of efficiency, it is now recognized as organizationally primitive. To the extent that it works at all, it does so by creating hundreds and sometimes even thousands of rules covering everything from haircuts to shoeshines and punishing failure to comply with those rules severely. The early chiefs recognized the punitive possibilities of such an administrative structure and welcomed it as a way of weeding out of police ranks the lazy, the incompetent, the disobedient, and the corrupt. But beyond that punitive capacity, the military administrative model offered little more. (If it did, you can be sure that the offices of IBM, Xerox, and DuPont, not to mention Sony, Nissan, and Toyota, would be staffed with sergeants, lieutenants, captains, majors, and generals.) The central failing of the military administrative model is that it rests on the unwarranted assumption that employees will not soon figure out that the surest way to avoid being punished for doing something wrong is to do as little as possible. The administration can, in turn, respond by setting quotas for the minimal amount of work it will tolerate from employees before it moves to punish them, but if it does, that minimal amount of work is, by and large, all the administration will get.

CONFINED TO
PREVENTIVE PATROL

The third major way in which the original architects of the New Police sought to neutralize the political uses of their unarmed and uniformed constables was to confine them to patrol for the *prevention* of crime. This restriction was understood to have the effect of limiting the uniformed, patrolling constable to two relatively apolitical types of interventions:—situations in which they were called upon for help by citizens who approached them on the street, and situations that, from the street, they could see required their attention. This second type of intervention, the English believed, would be much rarer than the first not only because high visibility of the uniformed patrolling constable would make it likely that troublemakers would see him before he saw them, but also because the whole idea of the highly visible patrolling constable was that his presence should prevent street problems from arising.

In the early American police experience uniformed patrol served the principal purpose of imposing some semblance of order on unruly officers. Patrol offered some assurance that patrol offices could be found at least somewhere near the area to which they were assigned. In short, the uniformed patrol beat made it less possible for police officers to hide from citizens or from their sergeants. Although this was no small achievement in the history of early American policing, the adoption of patrol as the major way of getting American and English policing done has gone on to shape both institutions in profound ways.

Patrol and the Street. The first institutional consequence of adopting patrol as the major mechanism of getting policework done is that it makes the patrol officer's domain the street, building line to building line. And unless they are called inside, their patrol beat limits them to attending to much more. This rather modest observation has two major consequences. One is that because patrol officers' territory is the street, they have acquired a host of street-related responsibilities because they are the only state employees who can be counted on to be on the street 24 hours a day. It is for this reason that we give police responsibility for checking parking meters, monitoring the opening and closing times of pubs and taprooms, taking accident reports, monitoring road conditions, and myraid other activities that have nothing to do with the right to use force or are likely to require it. Nevertheless, the addition of these duties to patrol officers' responsibilities reinforces their assumption that whatever goes on in the street is their business.

Patrol Officers and the People They Police. The second major institutional consequence of making patrol officers' domain the street is that those people who spend their time on the street will receive a disproportionate amount of police attention. Everyone, of course, spends some time on the street, but certain classes of people spend much more time there than others. I have in mind particularly people who are too poor to have backyards, country clubs, summer homes, automobiles, air conditioning, or other advantages that are likely to take them out of the patrolman's sight. The fact that patrol by its very nature focuses police attention disproportionately upon the poor is no more true of American police than English police whose model of a "politically neutral" preventive patrol they adopted.

Patrol and Police Organization. The third major institutional consequence of patrol as the dominant method of American and British policing is that it forces an occupational structure on police agencies that looks something like a pyramid: very wide at the bottom and rapidly narrowing from there on up. What this shape means to patrol officers is that on their first day on the job they will be patrol officers and for most, if not all, of their police careers they will never be anything else. In the typical American police department, over 85% of line employees are assigned to uniformed patrol (Kansas City Police Department, 1971). This fact has nothing to do with the quasi-military organization of the police. It is the simple and unavoidable consequence of keeping patrol the major way of getting policework done.

Because police agencies must retain the vast majority of their employees in patrol duties, there are few rewards they can offer patrolmen. Few of the rewards they have to offer have anything to do with the skills of doing patrol work well. There is no reason to believe that the skills necessary for a good police administrator are the same as those for a good patrol officer. If they should happen to be present in the same individual, that happy combination is little more than a matter of chance. The relation between the talents necessary for good work in patrol and the skills necessary to perform well in special police roles, such as crime analysis, communications, records, and data processing, is even more remote. Thus even under the fairest of promotional systems, patrol officers may well find themselves working for supervisors who cannot do the jobs they ask patrol officers to do, or supervisors who know how to do a patrol officer's job but do not have the skills necessary to manage others properly doing it. In either case patrol officers who want to move up in the police hierarchy will find themselves trying to do patrol work well to show that they are capable of doing a good job at something entirely different. Patrol officers have a phrase that precisely captures the incompatibility between the kind of behavior that is required to be a good street cop and the kind of behavior that will serve the patrol officer who wants to move up in the organization: "You can't do the job and play the game at the same time."

But in policing some special features of the patrol work serve to sever the relationship between either the quantity or the quality of patrol work and promotion. For most of modern American police history, promotion as well as hiring and firing was almost exclusively a matter of one's relationship to the local political party in power. In most departments today, as a product of unionization, civil service, labor laws, and one type of appointment or promotional exam or another, this relation no longer pertains with regard to firing and pertains only indirectly with regard to hiring and promotion. By "indirectly" I mean that many departments are under some political pressure to hire and promote some mediocre recruits simply because they are black, Hispanic, or women and give special treatment to others who have close connections to people who pass on police department budgets or hire and fire police chiefs. To assume otherwise would be politically naive. What this means is that anyone who takes up a career in policing—and with very few exceptions this means starting out in patrol—must be prepared to witness at least some people move ahead of him or her who have no better qualification for doing so than a political connection. This patrol officers must do without, as police say, "going sour" or they will be of no use to themselves or the people they police. Those with connections will take up some proportion of scarce departmental rewards. What can be said about those who remain, beyond what has already been said about the differences in skills required for patrol, administration, and specialized services? Put differently, how can patrol officers show their supervisors that they are doing good work and gain recognition and possibly promotion for it? The answer is that doing so is very difficult. Most of the work patrol officers do takes place where no police supervisor can watch them do it and before witnesses (complainants, suspects, and perpetrators) who are not regarded as reliable evaluators of how well it is done. More important still to patrol officers' problems of showing that they are doing good work is that neither the quantity nor the quality of their work is measurable against any clear standard of what is "good." Is a domestic dispute settled in the "right" way by arresting an angry husband? Is an officer writing "too many" tickets or "too few"? Are patrol officers making "too few" pedestrian stops because they know the people in their patrol area or because they are lazy? Are they spending "too much" time on complaints, forcing others to cover their calls because they are "slow," or are they taking the time they do because they are making a special effort to deliver "good service"?

These questions are technically unanswerable. I do not mean by this either that they cannot be answered at all or that some answers are not more satisfactory than others. Police supervisors—patrol sergeants in particular—have to answer these and many other technically unanswerable questions each time they instruct or evaluate an officer under their command. By "technically unanswerable" I mean that such questions are fundamentally matters of value, of the *ends* of policing, of the moral and political visions different people may bring to policework. Although we can easily think of examples of "bad" policework, what, in any given situation, is "good" policework is often an open moral and political question. Under such conditions patrol officers should not be surprised to find themselves supervised and evaluated by a sergeant whose moral and political vision of "good" policework is radically at odds with their own.

CONCLUSIONS

This chapter began with the discovery that once policing was made a full-time, paid vocation the only means of controlling it that was not available for controlling avocational forms of policing was the option to dismiss—to fire police officers who behaved disobediently. Thus the key to understanding how and why the English and American police developed into such different organizations involves examining who in each system had the right to exercise the firing option and on what occasions and for what reasons they saw fit to use it. What we found was that from the beginning, English police administrators had full control over the option to dismiss disobedient or incompetent constables and that for much, if not most, of American police history police administrators had little control over the firing option because they were forced to share it with local politicians.

This situation presented English and American police with radically different political problems. The political problem of the architects of the New Police, who had control of the means necessary to create a highly disciplined organization, was to demonstrate that the organization would not be used as a weapon by the administrative branch of government to destroy civil liberties. To achieve this end, the architects of the New Police employed three major political controls: the New Police were kept *uniformed, unarmed,* and confined to *preventive patrol.*

The political problem of American police administrators was, by contrast, trying to run a police agency when virtually any everyday decision could be reversed by some local politician. Under such conditions, American police could not be controlled by anyone. Early American police resisted the control of the uniform and armed themselves in direct defiance of administrative orders. To gain control over the agencies they were supposed to administer, American police administrators employed a military, crime-fighting rhetoric that eventually succeeded in giving them the administrative control they needed. But in creating that image of a crime-fighting American police for their immediate political purposes, they created a host of long-term problems: a public expectation of what they could and did do that bore little relation to reality, a quasi-military organizational structure that is too punitive and too crude to be an effective means of supervising an occupation as varied and as subtle as policing, and an occupational hierarchy that has few rewards to offer, few of which require the same skills as good patrol work, and fewer still of which can be evaluated by any process that even approaches objectivity. Understandably, frustration, cynicism, secrecy, and disenchantment are common features of the occupational culture of modern policing.

DISCUSSION QUESTIONS

1. Suppose you were a police supervisor—or, better yet, a chief of police—and wished to develop an evaluation form for sergeants with which they would rate and rank the officers on their patrol platoons. What items would you include on the evaluation form, and what weight would you attach to each of them?

2. Would you consider giving a similar form to victims of crimes or citizens involved in incidents handled by patrol officers? How about to people officers had arrested? If so, what different items, if any, would you include on your patrol officer evaluation forms if you decide to distribute them to these groups?

NOTES

1. On the general admiration the English have had for their police see Geoffry Gorer, *Exploring English Character* (1955), in which he argues that since the middle of the nineteenth century the bobbie has represented the male character ideal for the general English population.

2. In 1887 slightly more than 50% of the Chicago police force was foreign-born Irish or of Irish parentage. As of 1913 2% of the Chicago police force was black. See Mark Haller (1976).

3. See the National Advisory Commission on Civil Disorders (1968:165-66, 199). As of the mid-1960s what inroads had been made by black and Hispanic police officers were still largely confined to the lowest ranks. Under affirmative action pressures during the 1970s, many departments took aggressive steps to recruit and retain minority applicants. See Isaac C. Hunt and Bernard Cohen, (1971). Despite these efforts, which included mobile recruitment vans in inner-city areas, storefront offices, presentations at high schools with high minority enrollments, and advertising in minority publications,

some departments (Chicago and Philadelphia, among others) actually suffered a net *loss* in minority representation from the levels reported in the late 1960s. A good part of this loss may be attributable to the attraction of minority candidates to more attractive positions in the private sector.

4. On the arming of the Boston police see Roger Lane (1967): 103-104, 134, 302); on the arming of the New York police see Richardson (1970:113) and Wilbur Miller (1977:49-54).

5. Robert Fogelson's *Big City Police* (1977: 40-66) is the best history of the political uses of the military metaphor.

4

SHAPING THE POLICE VOCATION: THE DETECTIVE

My theory is that people who don't like mystery stories are anarchists.

—Rex Stout

The largest library in the world—the Library of Congress in Washington, D.C.—covers 35 acres of floor space in which there are some 50 miles of shelves. If all the 311 million copies of the mystery books sold by just one author, Erle Stanley Gardner, were assembled in one place, they would fill the Library of Congress more than four times over. If all the 300 million published works of a second mystery writer, Agatha Christie, were added to Gardner's pile, they would fill another three buildings the size of the world's largest library. Of course, the Library of Congress does not hold all the copies sold of every single book. This is fortunate, if only because single copies of each of the 600 or so different books written by mystery writer John Creasy (under his own name and 26 *noms de plume*) already occupy more than 50 feet of shelf space, not to mention the additional 20 or so feet of shelf space that are required for the foreign language translations of Creasy's mystery stories.

What makes the detective so special? How did the detective role become the most celebrated role in modern police agencies and a cultural institution of gigantic proportions? How did the detective grow to become a genuine folk hero?

These are the questions we will take up in this chapter. They have been raised and answered before in many different ways.[1] But the work we have done in the first three chapters of this book will allow us to look at them in a new and rather different way. In particular, the idea of police we have developed so far obliges us to try to define the detective role in terms of its means. It encourages us to look at the obstacles that stood in the way of bringing detective work from the private to the public sector. It urges us to test detectives' receptivity to the control of firing them if they misbehave. Moreover, all the work we have done so far demands that we ask what assurances of political neutrality the idea of detective offered to allow it to escape the controls of the uniform, confinement to preventive patrol, and the martial discipline of the quasi-military police order, within which it stands as an obvious and extraordinary exception.

THE IDEA OF DETECTIVE

Let's begin our study of the idea of detective with a little mystery:

> *In 1829 and for fully a quarter of a century thereafter, no one, not a single person anywhere in all of England or anywhere else in the world, wanted any member of the New Police to be a "detective."*

If you are an active reader, by which I mean someone who reads and thinks at the same time, I suspect that you are thinking to yourself, "How can Klockars know that? How could he know that in 1829 *nobody* anywhere in the world wanted any member of the New Police to be a detective? Suppose some little old lady in East London thought it would be a good idea. Rubbish! That can't be true!"

Now, if you're saying that or something like it to yourself, you are exactly the kind of active reader I hope is reading this book. You are, however, wrong. I said exactly what I meant and what I said is true. You will find out why in the next paragraph, but before you look there read my apparently outrageous statement again and see if you can figure out what could possibly permit me to make it.

You didn't go back and read it again, did you? Well, no matter. The reason no one wanted any member of the New

Police to be a detective was that the word "detective" had not yet come into being. Although "detective" was possibly used as an adjective in spoken language as early as 1840, it did not appear in print as an adjective until 1843. "Detective" became a noun in the mid-1950s as a shortened form of the phrase "detective policeman."[2]

Why is all this talk about the origins of the word "detective" important to our understanding of what the idea of detective eventually comes to be? It points us to the simple fact that in the early 1840s the idea of detective had not been defined. Unlike you and me, in whom the word "detective" conjures up all sorts of images and expectations that influence what we think about detectives and how we behave toward them, the average citizen of London in the first half of the nineteenth century had no image of what this new type of police agent, "the detective," would be.

**The Architects and Artists of
the Idea of Detective**

Thus the problem of the architects of the New Police, Robert Peel, Charles Rowan, and especially Richard Mayne, was to construct an image for the new role of detective that would be acceptable to the public. These men were, however, not the only ones who were engaged in the task of creating an image for the new role. It was a task they would have to share with the artists of detective fiction, all of those writers who, beginning with Edgar Allen Poe, have helped that role and our images and expectations of what it is and can be.

Although the idea of detective only began to be defined late in the second quarter of the nineteenth century, the average citizen of London at that time was familiar with some avocational, private-sector police roles that did what the new detective would do: investigate crimes, apprehend criminals, and recover stolen property. But only one type did so for money, as the new detective would. I refer, of course, to entrepreneurial avocational police. In the early nineteenth century three particularly distasteful entrepreneurial avocational police roles captured the English imagination. There was first the *informer,* the police spy who betrayed those who trusted him. Next came the *thief taker,* the piece-rate mercenary who was skilled in blackmail, perjury, and receiving stolen property. Finally, there was the most contemptible of all, the *agent provocateur,* the police agent who led innocent persons into crime so he could turn around and arrest them for the reward their capture would bring.

A trick of definition makes it true that in the second quarter of the nineteenth century no one wanted any member of the New Police to be a detective, but no trick is necessary to assert that few, if any, wanted any detective to be an informer, thief taker, or *agent provocateur.* The architects of the role of the New Police detective and the artists of detective fiction shared the common problem of creating a detective role that would be acceptable to the public. In the early nineteenth century this meant showing the public that this new type of police officer, the detective, would not be just another name for an informer, thief taker, or *agent provocateur.*

THE DETECTIVE AND THE INFORMER

Of the three contemptible entrepreneurial avocational police roles detective would eventually have to overcome, the role of the informer posed the most difficult problem. It did so because what makes the informer so repugnant is a matter over which neither the architects of the real police detective nor the artists of detective fiction had any real control.

What is it that makes the informer so disliked? To answer this question, let's introduce a word that will allow us to distinguish between someone who gives information to the police and is despised for doing so and someone who gives information to the police and earns no disrespect for doing so. The word is *"informant."* It means simply someone who provides information, be it to the police or anyone else. *"Informer,"* by contrast, is also a word that means someone who provides information, but its use indicates that we disapprove of the person for having done so. In short, "informer" is always pejorative, while "informant" is evaluatively neutral.

Now let's look at two somewhat similar situations, one in which you would be likely to use the neutral word "informant" and the other the pejorative word "informer," to find out what it is about such situations that makes what informers do so objectionable.

Suppose you are walking down the street one evening. You see a car come speeding by, go out of control, hit a pedestrian, and speed off. You notice the license number of the vehicle and report it to the police, who eventually arrest and prosecute the hit-and-run driver on the basis of your testimony. In such a situation nobody I know would object to what you did. You would be an informant, not an informer.

By contrast, suppose you are walking down the street and see in a darkened alley two teenagers necking hot and heavy in a parked car. You notice the license number of the vehicle and report it to the police, who eventually arrive and arrest and prosecute the male for sexual misconduct. (Let's assume that he is 19 and she is 15).[3] In such a situation, many people would feel that what you had done was unnecessary or malicious meddling and would not hestitate to call you an informer.

What is the critical difference between these two incidents, and how does it help us understand what makes us dislike informers? In the hit-and-run case we feel neither hostility toward the law that makes it a crime to hit a pedestrian and drive away nor sympathy for the driver who did so. If people do that sort of thing, most people have no objection to punishing them for it. In the second case, many people, particularly young ones, are downright hostile to laws prohibiting sexual activity between young people. They tend to be sympathetic to persons prosecuted for that kind of criminality and find almost any kind of punishment for that type of offense to be unwarranted. So we can say that what makes inform*ants* inform*ers* is not merely that they give information to police, but that they do so in situations in which there is (1) hostility toward the law, (2) sympathy for the criminal, or (3) resistance to the state's intent to punish. One of the reasons the state usually has to pay informers is that under such conditions average citizens are just not willing to come forward with information.

This understanding of what it is about informers that makes them so objectionable helps us explain why certain countries at certain times in their history are not only full of informers but why the people of those countries are also truly outraged by their activities. A good example is Ireland. Probably no country in the world has more history, songs, ballads, literature, and folklore dramatizing the treacherous and traitorous behavior of police informers. Why? Because for a long time a significant proportion of the Irish people have opposed the rule of English law, been sympathetic to the Irish criminals who in acts of political resistance have broken it, and regarded those who broke that law as martyrs and heroes when they were caught and punished. Richard Mayne, who for 40 years served as the first commissioner of the New Police and was the most important architect of the image of the English police detective, was Irish. So was his co-commissioner, Charles Rowan. It is not unreasonable to suggest that because of their Irish origins they inherited a special sensitivity to the problem of distinguishing the new role of detective from the very old and very unpopular role of informer.[4]

Early Nineteenth-Century English Attitudes toward Crime, Criminals, and Punishment. At the beginning of the nineteenth century, under what has often been called "the Bloody Code," no less than 200 different offenses were punishable by the penalty of death. In a typical year in the first quarter of the century more than 10,000 people stood accused of some capital crime. Few, however, were found guilty and fewer still were executed. Juries often refused to convict persons who were obviously guilty because the punishment they would receive was so excessive. Moreover, victims were often reluctant to prosecute and witnesses were reluctant to come forward to testify for the same reason. Best estimates suggest that fewer than 15% of all the people who stood charged with capital crimes in the early nineteenth century were actually executed for them (Radzinowicz, 1957:151; Tobias, 1967:232-236).

The irony of this situation is that although Robert Peel could tell the House of Commons in 1830 that "capital punishments are more frequent and the criminal law more severe in this country than in any country in the world," the undue severity of the English criminal law created sympathy for offenders and rendered it impotent for their control. If we judge from conviction rates alone and fail to count the undoubtedly larger number of offenders victims were unwilling to bring to prosecution, it is fair to say that an agent of the state who brought a garden-variety criminal to punishment in the early nineteenth century and did so for a fee was, like the informer, likely to be regarded with contempt. What would have to happen before the detective could achieve broad-scale public support was a reformation of the English criminal law into a legal system the public would support.

The movement for reform of the Bloody Code came not only from those who opposed its severity on humanitarian grounds but, perhaps more important, from those who wanted a code and system of justice people would be willing to enforce. Reforms came rapidly and on many fronts. By the mid-1830s murder became virtually the only crime that was ever followed by execution. The penalties for literally hundreds of lesser crimes were substantially reduced. Along with the reduction of capital crimes came the elimination of many horrendous postexecution practices. The last beheading after hanging took place in 1820, the same year the law changed to prohibit the practice of publicly dissecting corpses after execution. Public executions were ended altogether in 1868.

Similar reforms took place with noncapital punishments. The pillory was abolished in 1816, public whippings by the mid-1820's. Imprisonment for debt was no longer possible after legal reforms of the 1860s. The Hulks, the brutal prison ships to which offenders were sentenced, were closed down in 1858, the same year in which the last convict ship departed for the colonies. Throughout the middle years of the century English prisons received a great deal of legislative and administrative attention, which had the effect of making at least some of them more efficient, less corrupt, and somewhat more humane than they had been in the first half of the century. In 1865, 1874 and 1877 Parliament enacted legislation that progressively *increased* prison discipline. That legislation signaled the end of popular unwillingness to punish. Thus by the end of the third quarter of the nineteenth century, anyone who brought a common criminal to justice might well expect popular approval.

But as we already know, detectives in name, in fact, and in fiction did not wait until public attitudes were fully willing to receive them to make their appearance. What they did do—or, more precisely, what the architects and artists of the idea of detective understood was necessary to have them do—was appear in special circumstances designed to overcome the public sentiments that stigmatized the informer. Two of these originally defensive conventions have gone on to become enduring parts of the idea of detective.

Murder. The most serious of offenses, murder, was and still is the crime on which fictional detectives are most always seen to work. Edgar Allen Poe used it as the crime in the first two detective stories "Murders in the Rue Morgue" (1841) and "The Mystery of Marie Roget" (1842). It is the crime Sherlock Holmes solved in his first case, "Study in Scarlet" (1887), and most of the others that followed it. The convention continues to this day. Be it Mike Hammer, Columbo, or even the fluffy Jonathan and Jennifer Hart, the detective's crime of choice always has been and, apparently, always will be murder.

It is no accident. The murderer is the criminal toward whom we are least likely to be sympathetic, the criminal whose capital punishment least offends us. Knowing this, the artists of detective fiction tied their detectives tightly to the crime of murder.

Murder and the New Police. For the same reasons, the architects of the idea of the New Police detective did so as well. They took the occasion of a particularly brutal murder and the fear and anger it aroused to announce the formation of their first small unit of "detective policemen." The announcement came late in 1842, after the murderer, a man named Danial Good, had been apprehended, tried, and executed. Good had killed his wife, dismembered her, and was in the process of burning her remains when he was discovered by a uniformed constable. He escaped from the constable and was not recaptured for about two weeks, during which time the press demanded his apprehension and criticized the New Police for their inability to do so. The timing of the announcement of the formation of the detective department was meant to suggest that situations like those of the Good case required the formation of a detective force. However, it is entirely possible that the new detectives were in existence throughout the entire case.[5] Whether they were or not, there is certainly no way they could have prevented the Good murder, and it is most unlikely that they would have apprehended him any sooner than the uniformed branch did.

After announcement of the formation of the eight-man detective department in 1842, no public notice of their involvement in another case is given until February 1845. The occasion was another newsworthy murder, the Hocker case, marked by unusually flamboyant trial testimony, great public interest, and the eventual execution of the murderer. Hocker was followed shortly by still another murder case in which detective talents were called into play. The victim was George Clarke, a police constable who was beaten to death and mutilated while on patrol. Detectives were not able to solve the Clarke case, but they turned up enough evidence to arrest Clarke's police sergeant and some of his fellow constables, though not enough to bring them to trial for Clarke's murder. Although the arrest of Clarke's sergeant and fellow constables did no good for the overall reputation of the New Police, it tended to show that the New Police detectives possessed a special integrity of purpose and institutional independence even in a case in which the results of their investigation meant public embarrassment for their employers.

Wrong Person. Because it is the most serious of crimes, murder helps the detective overcome informer problems: hostility to the law, sympathy for the criminal, and resistance to the state's intent to punish. There is, however, an even more powerful convention, *wrong person.* What wrong person does is involve the detective in freeing an innocent person who is wrongly accused of a crime. This the detective usually does by finding the truly guilty party. In combination with the convention of murder, the convention of wrong person is especially potent. Together they place the detective in the position of doing double duty: punishing the worst of criminals while saving an innocent from the worst of punishments.

Poe used the convention of wrong person in both "Murders in the Rue Morgue" and "The Mystery of Marie Roget." It is also found in a very famous early detective novel by Wilkie Collins, *Woman in White* (1860), a story about a woman whose relatives conspire to claim that she is dead and substitute the body of another woman in her place so that they may inherit all her worldly possessions except the white dress she is wearing. Doyle has Sherlock Holmes find the truly guilty party at least half a dozen cases in which a wrong person is accused.[6]

Although the convention of wrong person is very powerful and we can find it used often in modern detective fiction, it is not as common a convention as murder. One reason for this is that using the convention of wrong person requires the creation of a detective who will do battle with those agents of the state who have falsely accused and arrested the wrong person. In some detective stories authors do this by creating a police detective who is a rogue or maverick and is willing to defy the conclusions of police colleagues. But more often, using the convention of wrong person seems to require creation of a detective who is not an agent of the state but a *private agent*—a private citizen hired by the victim, the accused, or their friends or relatives to do what police detectives cannot or will not do.

THE DETECTIVE AND THE THIEF TAKER

Creating a detective who is a private agent, as was Sherlock Holmes and Poe's first fictional detective, Auguste Dupin, raises the problem of distinguishing the detective from the thief taker. If the new role of the detective merely meant someone who would solve crimes for a fee, what reason was there to suspect that the new detective would be any different from the contemptible thief takers?

To answer this question, let's look closely at the popular objections to the thief takers, excluding those that sprang from their all-too-common corruption of the role by perjury, blackmail, and entrapment. There were two types of objection to the thief taker role itself, both of which derived from understanding the thief takers' motive for work as nothing more than money. The first objection concerned the thief takers' collection of rewards for bringing felons to successful prosecution. Because thief takers' earnings were based upon the number of felons they managed to capture, it was usually uneconomic for them to undertake difficult or complicated cases or those that put them in danger or caused them considerable personal risk. What interested the thief takers as economic actors was not the seriousness of offenses, the public outcry for their solution, or the threat to the public posed by an offender who might strike again, but the probability of solution of a case weighed against the costs, risks, and rewards of solving it. In short, the economic basis of the thief takers' work provided them with no redeeming social motive for doing it and no basis for a dignity of occupation. This objection was at the root of the indignant observation that even the most famous of the thief takers, the Bow Street Runners, would refuse to undertake an investigation until they knew that payment from the state, a wealthy victim, or some other source would be forthcoming (Pringle, 1958, 1965).

The second objection to the thief takers found them too cozy with certain types of felons, particularly professional thieves and dealers in stolen property, "fences." Thief takers made their money not only from the arrest and capture of criminals but from recovering stolen property as well. They charged a fee for this service, usually a percentage of the value of the property they recovered. What many thief takers discovered was that by allowing certain fences and thieves to operate unmolested, they could act as brokers between them and their victims, collecting a percentage of the value of the stolen property and giving thieves and fences a ready market for its sale. Over the long run this proved to be a more lucrative and less dangerous way of doing business than arresting them.

It was these two objections that the old role of thief taker obliged the architects of the New Police detective and the artists of detective fiction to overcome.

Distinguishing the New Police Detective from the Thief Taker.
On the face of things it would seem that the architects of the

New Police detective stood in a far better position than the artists of detective fiction from which to counter thief taker objections. As full-time, salaried, public sector employees the New Police, detectives might be made to attend to crimes in the order of the social threat they posed, serve rich and poor alike, and remain unconcerned about the piece-rate earnings that caused thief takers to refuse to work and corrupt selective enforcement. The New Police detectives' promise might have been that they would work all cases "for free," by which, of course, we mean at taxpayers' expense.

It might have been the promise that distinguished the New Police detective from the thief taker, but it was not—at least not for 40 years after the first New Police detectives made their first appearance. They could hardly promise to work *all* cases with the eight detectives who formed the unit in 1842, nor could they do so when the unit was increased to 15 detectives in 1864. Even more important than the limitations their numbers placed upon what they could do was the fact that between 1842 and the early 1870s the New Police detectives sold their investigative services to private citizens, even though they were full-time salaried employees of the New Police. For 40 years the New Police detectives were *both* private and public sector employees.

The architects of the New Police—Sir Richard Mayne in particular—would undoubtedly have liked to arrange things differently. It is unthinkable that he would not have preferred to have his new detectives work exclusively for him, as opposed to having them divide their time between private and public sector work. Why then didn't he do so?

If Mayne had refused to let his detectives take on private sector work, they would not have remained New Police detectives for very long. After they had gained some experience and reputation as New Police detectives, they would have moved to the private sector where they could earn far more than their police salaries. Moreover, if Mayne had imposed exclusive public sector salaried work on his new detectives, soon he would have lost the only means of control over them that was gained by employing them on a full-time basis. I refer, of course, to the option of firing them, an option that is meaningful only if it constitutes a loss or penalty. It could hardly be considered a loss or penalty if dismissed detectives simply moved into the private sector and earned more than their public sector salaries. What Mayne could have done, of course, was create a very large detective division of 300-500 detectives. A detective division of this size that was paid only its state salary and worked all cases without charge might have eventually driven most private sector detectives out of business. But during this transition period in the face of public willingness to pay detectives for this kind of work, Mayne would have lost control of his detectives because the option to fire them would not have been meaningful.

Instead, Mayne chose a very cautious strategy. He brought into his detective service only men of sergeant rank or above. These men, Mayne knew, had higher salaries to lose if they were dismissed. Mayne also attempted to make assignment to the detective division temporary so that the men who worked there would not develop reputations as great detectives, which they could later market in the public sector. For more than a quarter of a century, until his retirement in 1869, Mayne kept his detective unit very small, supervised it personally, and balanced carefully their private and public sector earnings. Not once during all this time was there a single reported instance of corruption in Mayne's detective division.

But while Mayne's strategy kept his first detectives under tight control, it did not allow the detective division to grow to meet public needs. There was simply no way 10 to 15 detectives could meet all the needs for detective services in a city of nearly two million people. The task of expanding detective services fell to Mayne's successor, Sir Edmund Henderson. He enlarged the detective division to 200 officers. But within a few short years of doing so, he found his detective service embroiled in a major corruption scandal. In 1877 three of four of Henderson's chief inspectors of detectives were convicted of taking bribes from professional criminals in a scheme reminiscent of old thief taker tactics.

In 1878 the detective branch of the New Police was completely reorganized. The Criminal Investigation Division, the CID, was formed. Between 1878 and 1885 the number of New Police detectives was increased to about 800. Only by that time could the New Police make the only promise that would once and for all bury the old thief taker objections. As of 1885 what the New Police could say was that any serious crime that required detective attention would receive it at the state's expense. It was a promise to which the *private agents* of detective fiction would have to respond.

Private Agents and Detective Fiction. In 1852 in *Bleak House* Charles Dickens introduced the first New Police detective in English fiction, Inspector Bucket. Bucket was modeled after an actual New Police detective, Inspector Field, a friend of Dickens whose real-life exploits Dickens had dramatized on other occasions.[7] Bucket appears in *Bleak House* shorn up by the conventions of wrong person and murder, both of which he resolves by arresting the truly guilty party. He is as well a private agent, working the murder case for a fee. The same is true of the second New Police detective of English fiction, Wilkie Collins's Sergeant Cuff of *The Moonstone* (1868). Given what we now know about New Police detectives, it should come as no surprise that in neither of those very popular novels do their authors find it necessary to explain why their detective police heroes are working for fees.

But by 1887, nine years after the CID was formed with 200 detectives, and two years after the number of New Police detectives was increased to eight hundred, things were different and Arthur Conan Doyle knew it. He was obliged to spend a significant portion of the first section of his *Study in Scarlet* explaining how his private agent detective hero, Sherlock Holmes, earned his living by doing what New Police detectives did for free. Holmes's early explanations have gone on to become enduring conventions of the fictional detective myth.

Doyle realized that in order to charge a fee for what others are willing to do for free, at least two conditions have to be fulfilled. First, the work one charges for must, in some way, be "better" than the free work. This condition Holmes fulfills with the convention of *genius*. "No man lives or has ever lived," says Holmes in *Study in Scarlet* "who has brought the same amount of study and natural talent to the detection of crimes as I have done?"

Although it is a common convention of detective fiction, genius is not the only way to show that the private agent detective's work is better than that of the free competition. Another is to show that the free competition is incompetent, a convention I will call *invidious inadequacy*. It can be fulfilled by showing the state's police to be corrupt, lazy, merely unimaginative, or otherwise not up to the work required of them. In order to exercise this convention Doyle created Inspector Lastrade, one of many in a long line of police detectives whom private agent detectives could show to be worth just about what private citizens paid them.

What Doyle also understood about using the convention of private agent was that while the conventions of genius and invidious inadequacy could be used to show that the work of the private agent detective was better than the work of the free competition, he also had to fulfill a second condition. He had to show that the difference was worth paying for. Doyle handles this problem in many different ways. One, of course, is wrong person. Another is the convention of *master criminal*—Holmes's Dr. Moriarty, a criminal so skilled that catching him is beyond the modest talents of the public sector police. In fact, in *Study in Scarlet* Doyle has Holmes lament the fact that there are not enough master criminals around to challenge the genius of Holmes: "There is no crime to detect [nowadays], or at most some bungling villany with a motive so transparent that even a Scotland Yard official can see through it."

The problem of showing that the private agent detective's fee is worth paying for can be handled in still other ways. The convention of *wealthy victim* may be used. If victims or their friends or families are wealthy enough, they can be assumed to be indifferent to the matter of a fee. It is for this wealthy victim reason that we find so many classical detective stories set in castles, mansions, and other exotic settings frequented by the rich and super rich. But the problem can also be handled by making the detective indifferent to the matter of a fee. This can be done by making the detective an *expert amateur* rather than someone who earns his or her living from detective work. Lord Peter Wimsey solves murders as he lives off his inheritance. Mrs. Marple does so as she collects her modest pension. Jennifer and Jonathan Hart live off the profits of Hart Enterprises and would not dream of charging a fee for their services. And G.K. Chesterton's famous priest detective, Father Brown, has not only taken a vow of poverty but has his needs provided by his church. In a particularly ingenious manipulation of the convention of expert amateur, detective Ellery Queen can afford to spend his time solving murders because he can chalk his free detective work up to research for his main occupation—writing mystery stories. Still another way to handle the problem of the private agent's fee is to make him a *consultant* to the police, a private citizen employed by the police when they run into cases too difficult for them to handle. In 1887 in *Study in Scarlet,* Holmes claims to have been the only "consulting detective" in the world. Poe's Dupin preceded him in that role by nearly half a century.

Although all of these conventions are common enough ways of making the payment of a fee to a private agent detective unimportant, my impression is that the most common ways involve presenting the detective with a situation in which honor, decency, loyalty, or friendship oblige him to take a personal interest. The detective may be approached by a *sympathetic stranger* or a *damsel in distress* or called upon to help or avenge a *friend wronged.*

If we assemble all the conventions of detective fiction we have discovered so far—*murder, wrong person, private agent, invidious inadequacy, master criminal, wealthy victim, expert amateur, consultant, sympathetic stranger, damsel in distress,* or *friend wronged*—we will have described those parts of the modern detective myth that originally sprang up in response to long-standing objections to the despised roles of the informer and thief taker. There are undoubtedly other conventions that a more detailed or extend consideration of the evolution of the idea of detective could uncover. However, I must point out that although every one of the conventions I have identified is an important and enduring device in generating and sustaining the detective myth, not one of them is absolutely essential to it. It is possible to write a detective story or to envision a real police detective without using any of the conventions. The reason this is so is that we have yet to discover the convention that defines the detective—the convention without which there can be no detectives, real or fictional. To discover what it is, where it came from, and where it leads us, we must distinguish the detective from the *agent provocateur.*

THE DETECTIVE AND
THE AGENT PROVOCATEUR

Agent provocateur is a French term for which there is no wholly satisfactory English equivalent. But during the first third of the nineteenth century, "thief *maker,*" "blood money conspiracy," and "Popay" all served to bring the term's foreign meaning home. Thief maker was a long-standing charge against thief takers, a charge nearly as old as the occupation itself.[8] It took recognition of the various devices of deceit—perjury, entrapment, seduction, and false witness—by which thief takers induced innocents to crime or its appearance. "Blood money conspiracy" was a name given to describe the organized creation of criminals for profit. A phrase of mid-eighteenth-century origins, it was revived with a passion in 1816 when a group of four private entrepreneurial policemen, one of whom was a member of the famous Bow Street Runners, were tried, convicted, and executed for thief making. They had led three juveniles into a counterfeit scheme. Only after the boys had been convicted and sentenced to death was the entrapment plot uncovered.[9] Blood money conspiracy went further than thief-maker because it emphasized that often the thief makers earned their money at the cost of their victims' lives. "Popay," you will recall, brought home the fact that the *agent provocateur*'s motives could be personal or political as well as financial.

How could the architects of the role of the New Police detective and the artists of detective fiction distinguish the idea of the detective from the idea of the *agent provocateur?* What could prevent the new detective from creating crimes and criminals for personal, political, or financial reasons? One way to do so would be to create in the detective role controls that would bar detectives from using the deceptions, lies, and deceits necessary to the work of the *agent provocateur*. They could have, for example, put their detectives in distinctive police uniforms and confined their movements to patrolling regularly designated areas. Both of these controls would have virtually eliminated the possibility that detectives might engage in the deceptions and entrapment schemes of the *agent provocateur*. Had they done so, of course, they would not have created detectives but ordinary patrolling constables.

What the architects and artists of the idea of the detective did do was control detectives' use of deceptions and entrapment by giving them something the patrolling constables did not have: a *case*. The single universal convention of detective fiction and the defining attribute of the idea of the detective, case imposed a temporal barrier between the detective and the crime. A case begins, comes into being, *after* a crime is committed and *after* a criminal already exists. To use modern terminology, case makes detectives "reactive" rather than "proactive" investigators (Reiss, 1971). This simple sequencing of events in time prevents the detective from creating either the crime or the criminal as it presents him with the problem of *whodunit?*

The Detective and the Case

Despite the fact that case could and would go on to refute *agent provocateur* objections to the idea of detective, it could not do so overnight. What the public had to come to appreciate was that the idea of case and detective were inseparable. Detectives would have to become attached to their cases, evaluated in terms of their success or failure in solving them, and distinguished from other types of ununiformed police (e.g., vice officers) who were not reactive and whose work was not structured in terms of case. By keeping his first detective unit very small and assigning his first detectives only to the most serious and highly publicized crimes of the day, Mayne made it virtually unthinkable that his tiny group of detectives would have time for anything else but casework. Likewise, the artists of detective fiction in every case from "Murders in the Rue Morgue" to the most recent episode of *Hart to Hart* have tied their detectives to the problem of solving cases.

The connection of the idea of detective to the concept of case makes the detective a radically different kind of police officer than the uniformed, patrolling constable. Case gives to detectives two major rights uniformed patrol officers do not appear to have. The first is the right to organize and control how they spend their working time. Patrol officers, tied to a patrol beat, are responsible for attending to problems that arise on their beats more or less in the order in which they arise. With respect to control over where and when and how they spend their working time, patrolling constables are very much like workers on an assembly line. They have to be on the line and attend to jobs in the same order in which they occur. In patrol, work time is structured by *place* and what goes on there. This gives to patrol officers what one sociologist has called a "production" distribution of their working time (Zerubavel, 1981). It is a distribution of time characteristic of low-status, salaried workers and hourly employees. In contrast, the rights to case give detectives a "professional" distribution of their working time. It is the kind of control over their working time that doctors, lawyers, scientists, and other professionals enjoy. What it means is that detectives are, within limits, free to work cases in the order and to the extent that they determine attention is required. They can choose to put in more time on one case than another, work a recent case before an earlier one, postpone work on a given case, or set aside times of the day or week when they will not work any cases at all.

The second major right the case confers on detectives that profoundly distinguishes them from patrolling constables is an enormous measure of personal discretion. The more that case was seen to be the special personal responsibility of detectives and case solution a measure of the personal resources and talents individual detectives brought to their cases, the more personal discretion had to be accorded to individual detectives. Detectives could not reasonably be held individually responsible for solving their cases unless they were also given the personal discretionary freedom to do what was necessary to solve them. Whereas uniformed, patrolling constables could have their working personalities, their manners, and their movements dictated by department policy, detectives' casework responsibilities required that they be given individual discretionary rights that the architects of the New Police would have considered unthinkable for their patrolling constables.

The long-term consequence of the decision to lock detectives to the idea of case and to give them the freedom and status that the rights of case confer has been to create in the detective role one of the most desirable assignments in modern police agencies. No other line role is more sought after by patrol officers. What they know is that becoming a detective will not only confer upon them the public status of a professional, but it will also allow them to escape the controls of the uniform, quasi-military discipline, and confinement to demands of the place they have to patrol.

Detectives' control over their working time and their personal discretion set the stage for their rise to the status of individually distinctive professionals. But they fall short of accounting for the detective's rise to the status of a cultural hero. To understand that dimension of the idea of detective, it is necessary to examine the concept of case from a somewhat different angle and look at the means the detective employs to solve it.

The Moral Dimensions of Case

If it is constructed properly with all of its conventions arrayed in their right relations, the detective story is easy to read as a kind of morality play. When the detective's case involves murder or some other heinous offense, the freeing of an innocent person wrongly accused of a crime, a master criminal whom others are incapable of stopping, or a desperate plea for help from a friend wronged or a sympathetic stranger in dire straits, the case takes on a moral dimension. It takes it from its end: putting right some moral wrong. Under such conditions detectives are not merely doing a job or toying as expert amateurs with an intriguing puzzle. They are on a moral mission. If they solve their case, it is a moral victory, a victory for what is right and for everyone who believes that right should prevail. If not, it is a moral defeat and everyone who believes that good should triumph over evil loses.

Virtually every analysis of the cultural meaning of the detective story interprets it in this "morality play" way.[10] The problem with such an interpretation, however, is that all of the conventions that set up and sustain the detective story as a morality play in terms of its ends are subordinate and secondary to the means the detective uses to achieve them. The fact is that the detective's ends are not the principal interest of detective story readers, nor do they occupy the center stage in the detective story itself. What is of prime concern to the audience for detective stories and what occupies the most space and time in them are the methods and techniques—the means—the detective uses to discover and prove "whodunit." The principal interest in detective stories is not to see that a case is solved but to see how the detective solves it.

This is a rather subtle but important point, and in the face of moral ends as compelling as murder, wrong person, and master criminal it can be difficult to see. Perhaps the best illustration of it takes place in what is called the "inverted" detective story. This is a story in which the reader knows from the beginning "whodunit" and that the detective hero in the story will somehow manage to discover the identity of the culprit and prove his or her guilt. In conventional detective stories readers are kept in suspense about whodunit and fed clues that invite them to compete with the detective in solving the case. In an inverted detective story from the point of relevation onward, the story is an account of the ways the detective works to solve the case. The most familiar example of stories of this type are probably the cases of the first-rate television detective series *Columbo*. By placing the audience in a position in which it knows everything the detective is trying to discover, the inverted detective story focuses the entire interest in the story on the methods of the detective at the same time it exposes the attempts of whodunit to frustrate them. In short, the special lesson of the inverted detective story is that whodunits are not as much about whodunit as they are about the means by which those whodunit can be undone.

It is necessary to understand this rather subtle point about detective stories to see in them the special moral lesson they teach and their enormous appeal. It is not that murder is wrong. That point needs no emphasis and is so far removed from the daily experience of most readers of detective stories that it would be impossible to sustain an entire literary genre on that point alone. The moral lesson of detective fiction is far more general and more directly relevant to the daily lives and experiences of millions of consumers of detective fiction. It is that there are means within the grasp of everyone—logic, reason, careful observation, memory, study, and concentration—that if disciplined and cultivated, can be used to solve even the most difficult and apparently insoluble problems.[11]

It is hard to imagine a moral lesson that the middle-class audience for detective fiction—the doctors, lawyers, teachers, civil servants, scientists, engineers, composers, writers, bankers, ministers, and librarians—would more want to hear. In their daily lives all of them confront problems and difficulties and all of them have made heavy investments in mental means of solving them. It is precisely because Dupin, Holmes, Poirot, Queen, Wolfe, and Columbo employ the same mental means at their work that the respectable middle classes do at theirs that makes it possible for the readers of detective fiction to appreciate and compete with their detective heroes. Each time they do the moral lesson of detective fiction is repeated: The way to triumph over problems is through the disciplined application of the mental means at your disposal.

It is this moral lesson about the power and virtue of mental means that makes detective heroes like Dupin, Holmes, Poirot, Queen, Wolfe, and Columbo—the heroes of what is called the *classical* detective story—cultural and institutional heroes. Their victories celebrate the power and virtue of the morally exemplary mental means that our culture and its institutions hold most sacred. They are the means we teach our children to use to resolve disputes and solve problems, the civilized means our schools and universities are dedicated to cultivating, the noble means upon which science, scholarship, invention, and the very idea of democracy are based.

The "Adult" or "Hard-Boiled" Detective. There is, however, another kind of detective story with a another kind of detective hero who in his means teaches quite another moral lesson. Born in the days of Prohibition and the Great Depression and continuing to the present day, it is a distinctively American creation. I refer, of course, to "adult" or "hard-boiled" detective stories and their two-fisted heroes: men like Philip Marlowe, Lew Archer, The Op, Sam Spade, Mike Hammer, and Harry "Dirty Harry" Callahan. Although these detective heroes were impressively "street smart," they did not confine themselves to the exclusive use of mental means, nor did they lead lives dedicated to the cultivation of their mental capacities. They were men with appetites for women and whisky, and their success in solving cases was often as much a product of their ability to dish out violence as it was to take it.

In the means they used to solve their cases they taught a moral lesson that was in direct conflict with the moral lesson of the classical detectives. What the hard-boiled, adult detective heroes taught was that morally exemplary mental means were not enough to meet the demands of real-world cases. In the real, rough, hard, and grown-up world cases sometimes required the hard-boiled detective to resort to downright dirty means: to lies, seductions, threats, and violence. In effect, their message was that Holmes, Poirot, Queen, Wolfe, Columbo, and their like would not last ten minutes on the mean streets the hard-boiled detectives worked. What the hard-boiled, adult detectives argued was that the classical detectives' moral teaching was a fraud, a stork story for children and the genteel middle classes.

Whereas the classical detective is a cultural and institutional hero, the hard-boiled, adult detective is moral individualist. Willing to break the cultural and institutional rules that limit the classical detective to the use of morally exemplary mental means, the hard-boiled detective fashions his moral choices about what means to use to solve his case by drawing upon an inner reserve of character. The hard-boiled detective is a spiritual hero, a man whose personal code of dignity and honor, whose inward sense of right and wrong, leads him to do what is right even if doing so requires him to resort to morally dangerous, dirty, or illegal means.

At their deepest, most profound, and most abstract levels the classical and adult detectives embody radically different moral positions. The classical detectives live by a morality of *means*. In the language of philosophers they would be called "deontologists." The deontological position is most commonly associated with religious ethics, but it is also the kind of position the law takes in regulating social conduct. In moralities of this type we find flat injunctions against the use of certain means (e.g., "Thou shalt not kill." "Thou shalt not steal."). What the cases of the classical detectives attempt to demonstrate is that good ends can always be achieved through the talented, disciplined, and creative application of good means. The classical detective does not resort to dirty or illegal means. The classical detective plays by society's rules.

In the language of philosophers, the adult, hard-boiled detectives are "consequentialists." Theirs is an ethic of *ends,* and their cases evidence their belief that the rightness or wrongness of the use of any means can be judged only in terms of its consequences. They are fully prepared to use morally dangerous, dirty, and illegal means—to bend or break any rules—when the ends to be achieved through the use of such means are compelling enough to require them to do so.

Who is right, practically and morally? The "deontologist," morality-of-means classical detective or the "consequentialist," morality-of-ends adult detective? In the past decade major, nationwide research has demonstrated that the capacity of real police detectives to solve serious crimes is extremely limited (Chaiken et al., 1977). All but about 5% of serious crimes that are solved by detectives are solved because a patrol officer has caught the perpetrator at the scene, because a witness tells the detective whodunit, or by thoroughly routine clerical procedures. In a very small percentage of cases, perhaps 3%, extraordinary efforts by detectives may contribute to a case solution, but this is a far cry from the image the classical detectives promoted with their cases. Practically, by which I mean only what the evidence shows that real police detectives actually achieve in practice, the classical detective's promise—that even the most difficult of cases can be solved through the application of morally exemplary mental means—is a myth.

Morally, the classical detective's claim that good ends can always be achieved through the use of morally exemplary means is equally mythical. Morally dangerous, dirty, or illegal means can sometimes be used to achieve good ends and sometimes good ends cannot be achieved in any other way. This is why we give police the legal right to use and to threaten to use the morally dangerous means of coercive force, why, on some occasions, we permit them to use the morally dirty means of lying and deception, and why, on other occasions, they are morally inclined or obliged to ignore or break some of the legal rules we have set up to guide and restrain them. It is always preferable to use morally good means to achieve good ends, but sometimes good ends cannot be achieved without resorting to morally dangerous, dirty, or illegal means. Morally speaking, because good and decent and honest means cannot always be counted on to achieve good ends, we have police.

CONCLUSIONS

In this chapter we took up the problem of understanding how the detective, at one time the most suspect and distrusted of police roles, grew to become one of the most sought-after assignments in modern police agencies and a fictional figure of gigantic proportions. What we found was that the creators of the detective role, the architects of the New Police detective and the artists of detective fiction, shared a set of common problems. Most important, they had to distinguish the new role of detective from three very unpopular entrepreneurial avocational police roles: the informer, the thief taker, and the *agent provocateur*.

In dealing with these common problems the architects and artists of the idea of detective reached a number of similar solutions. In order to overcome informer objections, which stemmed from popular hostility to the undue severity of the criminal law and generated sympathy for criminals, both the architects and artists of the idea of detective tied it closely to the crime of murder. In dealing with thief taker objections, which stemmed from the thief takers' unwillingness to work cases unless adequate fees were assured, both the artists and the architects of the idea of detective developed ways of having their detectives work cases at no cost to the victim or complainant. State-salaried New Police detectives did some work of this kind from the time they came into existence, but the architects of the role of the New Police detective were not able to get them to work all cases at public expense until late in the nineteenth century. The artists of detective fiction were able to have their private agent detectives work cases without charge by making them state-paid consultants and expert amateurs of modest needs or independent wealth or by having them become involved in cases through special interests or special pleas from victims, friends of victims, or persons wrongly accused of crimes. In overcoming *agent provocateur* objections to the role of detective both the architects of the real police detective and the artists of detective fiction employed the convention of case. Case defines detectives, makes them reactive to complaints of crime, and in doing so prevents them from acting as *agents provocateur.*

Case also structures detectives' work in ways that are radically different from the way patrolmen's work is structured. Tied to the place they are assigned to work, patrolmen acquire a "production" distribution of their work time. Like workers on an assembly line, patrol officers are required to be at a given place for a given time and attend to the work that must be done in that place more or less in the order in which it arises. By contrast, the working world of detectives is structured by cases and the personal autonomy they must given to solve them. Case gives detectives a "professional" distribution of their work time and an enormous amount of individual discretion in how they use that time.

Although the freedom casework gives detectives prepared their way for the rise to professional status, it is the means detectives use to solve their cases that gives them their tremendous popular appeal. The "classical" detectives (e.g., Dupin, Holmes, Poirot, Columbo) embody one of the most profound hopes of Western democratic culture: that the creative, disciplined, and determined application of morally exemplary mental means can triumph over even the most skilled and sinister of evils. The "adult" of "hard-boiled" detectives (e.g., Mike Hammer, Sam Spade, Lew Archer, "Dirty Harry" Callahan), freed from the illusion that all evils will yield to the application of morally exemplary means, draw upon inner reserves of personal honor and character that allow them to judge when to use morally dangerous or downright dirty means.

At their deepest levels each variety of detective fiction thus occupies a polar position on how moral decisions are to be resolved. The classical detectives celebrate the virtues of the deontological position, the position associated most closely with religious ethics and legal rulemaking, which holds that there are means that are wrong in themselves and that the moral person must never use. The hard-boiled, adult detectives are consummate consequentialists, justifying their choice of means in terms of the results produced.

The conflict between the moral positions of the classical and adult detectives is dramatic. But it is important that you understand it as more than just a literary or philosophical controversy. It is at the very heart of the idea of police and the problems of controlling them. The fact is that we give to police the right to use morally dangeorus, dirty, and illegal means to achieve good ends because the most profound aspirations of our culture and its most noble institutions do not contain the means necessary to ensure their survival. Police, the only domestic occupation to which we give the right to use the morally dangerous and dirty means of coercive force and fraud, exist because of all the morally respectable and civilized means of handling problems and overcoming difficulties are simply not up to the task.

In the next chapter we will begin to take up the problem of the day-to-day control of police, the problem of police discretion, by examining the single most widely accepted illusion that we are doing so: instructing them to enforce the law.

DISCUSSION QUESTIONS

In this chapter I have made the case that the classical detective myth is a "stork story," a fairy tale we tell to children, big and little, because they are not mature enough to handle the truth. Is there a sense in which society needs such ennobling myths and cannot do without them? If so, are adult detective stories morally and culturally subversive? Is this chapter, which argues that the moral claim that good ends can be achieved only through good means is a fraud, subversive as well? Is it irresponsible to teach such a lesson to beginning students of police?

NOTES

1. Among the most worthy treatments of the question are A. E. Murch (1958), Ian Ousby (1976), Howard Haycraft (1946), Francis M. Nevins, Jr. (1970), David Madden (1968), Philip Durham (1963), William Ruehlman (1974), and John G. Cawelti (1976).

2. According to the *Oxford English Dictionary*, James A. H. Murray (Ed.) *A New Dictionary on Historical Principles* (Oxford: Clarendon Press, 1897, Vol. 3, p. 266), the adjective first appears in print in 1843 when Sir James Graham, then Home Secretary, announced that a few "especially intelligent men have been recently selected to form a body called the 'detective police' ," adding that "at times the detective policeman attires himself in the dress of ordinary individuals." It is relatively certain that the adjective "detective" was used in spoken language a few years prior to 1843. The noun form backs into the language as a shortened form of "detective policeman," appearing first in print in 1856. Eventually the noun form captured all the criminal, artful, occupational, and otherwise human connotations of the far older (1605) noun "detector," leaving it by the end of the century with a meaning reserved exclusively for things mechanical (e.g., metal detector).

3. The "age of consent" varies from state to state, but in the state in which I live (Delaware), the situation described constitutes a felony, punishable by a prison sentence of up to seven years and a fine or other conditions the court may order. The Delaware law (*Delaware Code Annotated* Rev. 1974, Title ii, sec.762, p. 63) reads:

A male is guilty of sexual misconduct when he engages in sexual intercourse with a female not his wife who is less than 16 years old and he is at least 4 years older.

4. In 1843 both Mayne and Rowan appeared before a Select Committee of Parliament to urge that private informing for profit be eliminated by a law that would give sworn police constables and victims of crime and their families a monopoly on the right to lay information for a warrant for arrest. Not only was their recommendation not enacted, but over the next 50 years, 47 new statutes were enacted that extended various privileges and rights of reward to private sector informers. All of these statutes were finally revoked in 1951 with the passage of the Common Informers Act (14 & 15 Geo. 6, c. 39).

5. The claim is made in the book, *The First Detectives and the Early Career of Richard Mayne, Commissioner of Police* (1957) but without any documented, evidentiary support.

6. Wrong person is a theme in "The Sign of Four," "The Boscombe Valley Mystery," "Thor Bridge," "The Beryl Coronet," "The Five Orange Pips," and in a number of Holmes's cases Watson mentions but does not discuss.

7. In 1850 Charles Dickens began a weekly magazine called *Household Words*. In it he published his two-part article "A Detective Police Party" and his "Three Detective Anecdotes" as well as an article he wrote with his co-editor, W. H. Wills, entitled "The Metropolitan Protectives" (Apr. 26, 1851).

8. It appears at least as early as 1718 in a pamphlet written by Charles Hitchen entitled "A True Discovery of the Conduct of Thief Takers, In and About the City of London." Hitchen was Under-City Marshal of London, and his pamphlet is directed at the famous thief-taker, Jonathan Wild. See Gerald Howson (1971).

9. On this and other "blood money conspiracies" see Radzinowicz (1957: 326-332) and Pringle (1958:97-140).

10. This is true of interpretations of both classical and adult detective stories. See W. H. Auden's "The Guilty Vicarage" (1956:146-158) and Raymond Chandler (1972:1-22), as well as the materials cited in note 1.

11. For what other reason than to emphasize this point could there be for Doyle's creation of Sherlock's businessman brother, Mycroft Holmes? Sherlock says of him during the case of the "Bruce-Partington Plans":

He has the tidiest and most orderly brain, with the greatest capacity for storing facts, of any man living. The great powers I have turned to the detection of crime he has used for this particular business. The conclusions of every department are passed to him, and he is the central exchange, the clearing-house, which makes out the balance. All other men are specialists, but his specialism is omniscience.

5

SELECTIVE ENFORCEMENT

In framing a government which is to be administered by men over men, the great difficulty lies in this: you must first enable the government to control the governed; and in the next place oblige it to control itself. A dependence on the people is, no doubt, the primary control on government; but experience has taught mankind the necessity of auxiliary precautions.

—*James Madison*

If visitors from another planet, anxious to learn our ways, asked us to explain how our police behave, perhaps the most unhelpful thing we could do would be to hand them a copy of our legal code and say "Our police enforce these laws." What would make this bit of bad advice so terribly unhelpful is its failure to recognize the enormous range of police discretion, which, far more than legal codes, shapes the way our police behave.

In this chapter I will try to do five important things. First, I will define police discretion. Second, I will show why police are inclined to minimize or even deny the importance of their enormous powers of discretion. Third, I will show why it always has been and always will be the most important factor in explaining police behavior, why it is absolutely essential, and why it cannot be eliminated. Fourth, I will identify some of the forces that influence police in making one type of discretionary decision: the decision *not* to make an arrest when there is sufficient evidence to do so. Fifth, I will review some ways of trying to get police to make better discretionary decisions than they currently do.

A Definition of Police Discretion

A police officer or police agency may be said to exercise discretion whenever effective limits on his, her, or its power leave the officer or agency free to make choices among possible courses of action or inaction.

There are other ways of defining police discretion, but this one, taken with minor modifications from Kenneth Culp Davis's book *Discretionary Justice* (1969) is the best known and most widely accepted.[1] At least three components of Davis's definition are worth emphasizing.

First, you will note that it identifies discretion as something that both an individual police officer or a police agency may exercise. It is crucial to understand police discretion not simply as a question of the choices police officers on the street make in the course of their everyday work, but also as a matter of the decisions and policies police administrators make that influence police behavior and allocate agency resources into one type of activity as opposed to another. In this chapter I am going to concentrate on a single type of discretionary decision: selective enforcement. But beginning with Davis's defintion, I urge you to remember that police agencies also make important discretionary decisions in many other ways: when they decide where to deploy personnel, what to teach recruits in the police academy, how to handle citizen complaints, and when to reward or punish police officers for their conduct. Each of these administrative decisions and a hundred others like them are highly discretionary and can profoundly affect the quality of life in a community.

Second, Davis's definition identifies decisions as discretionary insofar as a police officer or police agency retains the power to make them. This is not to say that police discretionary decisions are not influenced by other powers or forces outside the police agency, but that a police decision is discretionary insofar as the ultimate decision—even in the face of opposition—remains a police decision. Most police discretionary decisions are not reviewed or evaluated by anyone other than police themselves.

A third and final important feature of Davis's definition
is its emphasis on "action or inaction." Some police discretionary decisions are announced publicly and advertised as matters of policy, but many, if not most, are matters over which
police exercise their discretion by *not* doing something or by
failing to consider alternative ways of doing it. These types
of discretionary decisions have low visibility, are sometimes
intentionally concealed from public scrutiny, and are consequently especially difficult to influence or control. Most police
arrests are reviewed in some form of preliminary hearing, but
review of police decisions *not* to arrest is virtually nonexistent.

Why Police Discretion?

If this book were about doctors, lawyers, judges, scholars,
or scientists, or even if it were simply about police detectives,
it is extremely unlikely that there would be anywhere in it a
section entitled "Why Medical (or Legal or Judicial or Scholarly
or Scientific or Investigative) Discretion?" There would not
be such a section not only because everyone already knows
that all these professionals routinely exercise discretion but also
because everyone thinks that the fact that they do exercise discretion is a good and necessary thing.

Things are, of course, quite different when the question turns
to police. Only within the past 20 years have we really learned
how widely discretionary police behavior can be, is, and has
to be.[2] Yet, even today, many police agencies minimize or deny
the existence of their enormous powers of discretion, many
politicians behave toward police as if they had very little discretion at all, and most citizens are under the impression that
the job of police is simply to enforce the law. They have a
number of good reasons for doing so.

Full-Enforcement Statutes. Most states have some form of
"full-enforcement statute," a law providing that police shall
enforce *all* laws.[3] These full-enforcement statutes themselves
are rarely enforced, but they clearly make it the duty of police
to enforce *every* law relating to the safety of persons or property.

Although there is some debate in legal circles on the question, in states with full-enforcement statutes it appears that selective enforcement of the law is illegal by statute.[4]

Separation of Powers. The vast majority of states, in imitation of the federal government, separate the powers of government into three separate and distinct branches: the executive, the legislative, and the judicial. As every grade-school civics text explains, the power of each separate branch is limited and each branch's rights and duties are kept distinct from those of the others in order that a system of checks and balances be preserved. Selective enforcement of the law, by which I mean a police decision *not* to enforce a law that the legislative branch has passed, usurps the legislature's rights and violates the principle of separation of governmental powers. In the words of one critic of selective enforcement, "The police. . . purpose is to enforce prohibitions articulated by the legislature. We do not say to police: 'Here is the problem. Deal with it.' We say: 'Here is a detailed code. Enforce it' " (Allen, 1976:97).

A Government of Laws. At the heart of the "separation of powers" objection to police discretion is the contention that ours is a government of laws, not men. Under a government of laws the police should not be allowed to make what amounts to their own laws, amend laws that have already been made, or decide that some people should have certain laws enforced on them while allowing others to violate the same laws with impunity. The whole idea of police enjoying such broad discretionary powers seems to open the door to arbitrarines, favoritism, and discrimination. As one police chief put it:

A police officer does not have the discretion to arrest or not to arrest any more than a judge has the discretion judge or not to judge. . . . When some people advocate the philosophy that a police officer has discretion in the field to arrest an individual or to take him home, they are talking about *discriminatory law enforcement* which is *police corruption* [Archuleta, 1974:74, quoted in Goldstein, 1977:126].

In light of these three strong objections to the whole idea of police discretion in selective enforcement, it might seem to be a good idea to try to eliminate it entirely. But before you jump to that conclusion you should consider the counterarguments. If you have ever been stopped for a traffic violation and managed to talk your way out of getting a ticket—or think you should have been able to—you might be inclined to appreciate that at least on some occasions, police discretion might be a good thing.

Enforcing The Law

There are some kinds of police discretion in enforcing the law to which, in principle, no one objects. In every instance of law enforcement police have to make a decision that a violation of the law actually occurred and that there is sufficient factual reason to believe that a particular person was the one who did it. No one disagrees that police should make discretionary decisions of this kind, nor does anyone disagree that certain types of laws are written in such general terms (those prohibiting "reckless" or "inattentive" driving or "disorderly" conduct, for instance) that they require heavy interpretation by police before they can be applied to any given situation. In some situations police may make errors in application of the law, but even the staunchest critics of selective enforcement accept that discretionary decisions of this type must be made by police. *The real controversy over selective enforcement is about police decisions not to arrest when they have every right and all the legal evidence necessary to do so.*

In making the case for police discretion in selective enforcement it will be helpful to examine a law that is familiar, simple, and unambiguous. Why? Because such a law will permit me to demonstrate that even the most simple, familiar, straightforward, and unambiguous of laws requires selective enforcement. The law I would like to consider specifies that on a given stretch of road no motorist may travel legally in excess of 35 miles per hour. What law could be more familiar, simple, or unambiguous than that?

Now, let's see what you could say to a reasonable police officer who clocks you doing 50 miles per hour in a 35 mile per hour zone to get out of being cited when there all the legal evidence necessary for the officer to do so? I can think of at least ten good excuses under the following heading:

"Where's the Fire?"

THE OVERREACH OF THE LAW

(1) I am a volunteer fireman responding to a fire alarm.

(2) I am a volunteer ambulance driver responding to a call.

(3) I am an undercover cop tailing the car ahead which you did not stop.

(4) My wife just called and told me to rush home. She is starting to have her baby.

(5) I am having a baby.

(6) I am on my way to the hospital. There has been an accident. My child was hurt.

(7) I am on my way home. I left for work a short while ago, but halfway there I remembered that I left a steam iron burning on the kitchen table.

(8) I am on my way home. I left for work a short while ago, but halfway there I discovered I have a serious case of diarrhea.

(9) I am a school crossing guard. I am late for work because I just had a flat tire. If I don't get to my post right away, the children will try to cross a dangerous intersection by themselves.

(10) I am part of a funeral entourage on its way to the cemetery. I do not know the way to get there and a few blocks back I got separated. Unless I catch up I will miss the burial.

Many other excuses of this type are possible. But what you should understand about those listed above is that each of them makes a somewhat different kind of claim that the 35 mph speed limit law is written so broadly that it includes all kinds of situations that should be exempt from it. Each claims in a different way that the law as written *overreaches:* It includes cases that it ought to exempt. Furthermore, considering the range and variety of exemptions that just these ten excuses claim, I think you will appreciate that no traffic law could be written in such a way as to anticipate all of the possible reasonable exemptions to it. But the point of this example goes beyond traffic law. Simply stated, it is that every law has the property of overreach, whether it provides penalties for traveling in excess of 35 mph on a given stretch of road, gambling, assault, burglary, robbery, or the killing of another human being. Police exercise discretion in the selective enforcement of all of these and every other law because it is in the very nature of all law to criminalize more than it intends.

**"I'm Sorry, Officer,
I'll Never Do It Again.":**

THE PURPOSE OF THE LAW

In addition to the fact that police discretion exists because the law overreaches and cannot be written so as to anticipate every reasonable exception to it, police discretion also exists because the law as written has a purpose that may, under certain circumstances, be amply served by not enforcing it. Consider the following appeals, apologies, and explanations from motorists clocked at 50 in a 35 mph zone:

(1) I'm sorry, officer. I've just come from my mother's funeral and I'm still kind of upset. I just didn't check my speedometer.

(2) I'm sorry, officer. I just got fired from my job. I don't know how I'm going to support my family. Please don't give me a ticket. I don't know how I'd get the money to pay it.

(3) I'm sorry, officer. I've never in my life been stopped before. I think I'm going to faint. (*Thud*)

(4) I'm sorry, officer, but the kids were yelling in one ear and my wife was hollering in the other, and I just didn't notice the limit dropped to 35.

(5) I'm sorry, officer. I've been driving for 25 years and I've never even received a parking ticket before. In fact, I teach the driver education class at Central High School. Could you please give me a break? If I get a ticket for speeding, I'll be the laughing stock of the whole school. I could even lose my job. Please officer, just this once.

None of these appeals claims that the law as written over-reaches. All of the violators admit they are wrong, but what they claim is that the punishment the law provides for its violation is unnecessary or excessive in their particular case. The law is not an end in itself. It is a means for achieving an end. The five appeals above play on the officer's willingness to understand the violator's particular predicament, imagine being in the same situation, and consider whether or not the purpose of the law will be well served by adding the pain of legal punishment to the pain already evident.

In practical terms, this type of excuse is probably less frequently successful in convincing traffic officers not to issue citations than the type of argument that claims overreach. This would appear to be so for at least three reasons. First, each assumes that for the officer to whom the appeal is being made the law has a purpose and its purpose has something to do with traffic safety. Some officers may not understand issuing a citation as having that purpose at all. They may understand it as a way of raising revenue for the city or as a means of satisfying a quota that proves to their supervisors they are working. They may even understand their ticket writing as a means of hurting types of people they do not like. If police officers understand their writing traffic tickets to have one or more of these primary purposes, violators' appeals to the traffic safety purpose of the law are likely to fall on deaf ears.

Second, because arguments about the law's alleged purpose in punishing depend heavily upon a police officer's willingness and ability to empathize with the predicament of a particular offender, some excuses will strike empathetic chords in some officers and not in others. You will note that all five of the hypothetical excuses involve everyday realities that a middle-class police officer might be likely to appreciate. It may well be that an appeal based upon the urgency of getting home before someone steals your welfare check or to be present when the piano movers arrived with your new Steinway concert grand would be less warmly received.

Third and finally, every police officer knows that if doing so will allow them to escape punishment, most people are prepared to lie through their teeth. (I suspect that you, dear reader, have already sized up all of the excuses listed so far with an eye toward using one or more of them if you should ever be stopped.) Thus the police officer's problem in selective enforcement is not simply to decide when the purpose of the law will be well served by sensitive leniency, but to avoid being played the fool while doing so.

"Why Aren't You Out Catching Rapists and Murderers?":

THE QUESTION OF PRIORITIES

Caught dead to rights and without any believable claim that the law overreaches or would be better served by nonenforcement in their case, traffic law violators often resort to challenging police priorities in enforcing laws. Every policeman of any experience has heard some violator claim that instead of arresting him the policeman should be out arresting some more serious offender. The claim will not get you out of a ticket, but it raises one of the most telling arguments in demonstrating the necessity of selective enforcement.

The fact is that police resources are limited. A choice to enforce one type of law—be it traffic, vice, burglary, robbery, rape, or murder—usually involves diverting resources from the enforcement of laws of another type. The more specialized a police agency becomes, the more it is divided up into units that work on only one type of problem, the more obvious are the agency's enforcement priorities. In and of itself the fact that police resources are limited forces police to make selective enforcement policies whether they openly admit them or not.

**"This is a 35 Mile Hour Zone?
You've Got to Be Kidding!":**

THE PROBLEM OF BAD LAWS

If you are a driver of any experience you have driven on roads where posted speed limits were obviously too slow, where the pace of normal traffic regularly exceeded posted speeds by 10 or 20 miles per hour, and where, you hope, police exercised necessary discretion in not enforcing the legal limits. The lesson of this experience is a very general one: The law is not infallible.

Legislatures sometimes enact laws that make sense and receive wide-scale support in some communities at some times and in some situations but are wholly inappropriate in others. In part at least, this is so because of the way lawmaking works. Often laws are made in response to a crisis that mobilizes public sentiment and puts pressure on law makers to "do something"—a mandate legislators often interpret as passing a law against it. This whole country is littered with unnecessary stop signs and stop lights that traffic authorities were forced to install following some tragic accident. Likewise, political pressures can force legislators to enact what they know are bad laws as a way of satisfying local interest groups. But what legislators also know is that when and where the interest for enforcement of laws is absent, police will not enforce them. Such laws may eventually be repealed. But for reasons I am sure you will appreciate, legislators usually prefer to let them die a slow and quiet police discretionary death.

The analogy between simple traffic law and general criminal law may be pushed at least one step further. All sorts of traffic laws are good and reasonable and deserve to be enforced under certain conditions. At times of heavy traffic, some rules—no U-turns, four-way stops, red lights, no left turn across an oncoming traffic lane—make eminent sense. But at three o'clock in the morning when the streets are bare and one can see that doing so will present no danger to anyone, rolling through a stop sign or a red light or making an illegal left or U-turn would hardly seem to merit an arrest. The same general point holds for other laws that are sensible and just at certain times, at certain places, and under certain circumstances but become bad law if they are taken seriously and enforced in others. A law prohibiting the carrying of a concealed deadly weapon (e.g., a knife) without a permit is a reasonable law and deserves enforcement on city streets. In the wilderness, on a hunting or fishing trip, it is a bad law.

**"It's about Time You Police
Did Something about Those Cars
That Come Racing through Here.
Before Somebody Gets Killed!":**

THE AWESOME POWER OF CITIZEN DISCRETION

To examine the fifth and last of the critical dimensions of discretionary selective enforcement in the case of a simple traffic law requires that we bring a third actor into our little scene: a citizen complainant. Citizen pressures for enforcement or nonenforcement of traffic laws regularly affect police discretionary decisions in indirect ways. Citizen pressures may get police to crack down on violations in a certain area or ease up in others. It is rather unusual for direct complainants to be present at the scene of speeding violations, but I will bring one in anyway. If you will forgive me this minor distortion of everyday reality, it will allow me to make an enormously important point: *The wishes of complainants are the single most important influence on police selective enforcement practice.*

Why? First of all, police are reactive. In the vast majority of cases the police do not choose what they will attend to: A complainant does. If we exclude motor vehicle code enforcement, over 90% of all the problems police attend to are in response to citizen requests for service.[5] Someone calls the cops to report some "ought-not-to-be-happening-and-about-which-something-ought-to-be-done-NOW" type of incident. Of course, this proportion varies from one type of police agency to another and within police agencies from one type of enforcement unit to another. Police agencies like the U.S. Customs Bureau and the their own rather than through citizen initiatives, as do vice and traffic units within local police agencies.

The reactive nature of policing makes police dependent upon citizen discretion before they can take action. A number of studies show that citizens frequently decide not to involve the police, even in cases of major crime. Best estimates suggest that about half of all violent crimes and about three-quarters of all property offenses are never reported to the police (National Crime Survey, 1977).

Second, the influence of citizen discretion on police selective enforcement discretion does not stop once the police are called and arrive at the scene. Research by Donald Black (1971) has shown that in 176 situations he studied in which a complainant was present and police had sufficient evidence to make an arrest, they made an arrest in about two-thirds of situations in which complainants did not express a preference one way or another for police to make an arrest. However, police made arrests in three-fourths of the situations in which the complainant wanted an arrest to be made. But the truly remarkable finding by Black is that when the complainant *did not* want police to make an arrest, they did so in only 10% of the cases in which they had every legal right to do so (1971: 1095).

Given the enormous influence of citizen discretion on police decisions not to arrest, Black and others have studied a number of factors that might influence police to respect some complainants' preferences and ignore or take less seriously those of others. Among the most important factors appears to be what Black calls the "relational distance" between the complainant and the suspect. The importance of a complainant's preference for an arrest increases when the complainant and suspect are strangers to one another and decreases when they are friends, neighbors, acquaintances, or family members. Apparently police believe that the closer the relationship between the complainant and the suspect, the more likely social rather than legal forces will work to repair their differences.

Not surprisingly, Black and others have also found that police give more credibility to complainants and respect their wishes for an arrest when they are civil and respectful to police. This appears to be especially the case when the suspect is hostile and disrespectful. Black found no evidence that the race of the complainant or the suspect or the police officer made any difference in police selective enforcement decisions.

In contrast to Black's findings, some empirical studies have showed that the race of the suspect was a factor in certain types of discretionary enforcement decisions. In a study of selective enforcement in 293 traffic violations (either moving violations or defective equipment violations) Richard Lundman (1979) found that while there were no overall significant differences in the rates at which police chose to cite black as opposed to white violators, police did appear to cite black violators somewhat more frequently at times of the month when there was a heavy demand on police to produce traffic arrests. Lundman's finding must be interpreted cautiously, however, because it is based on a rather small sample of black traffic arrests (29), only 17 of which were made under high pressure by supervisors to produce arrests.

Having said this much about police discretion in selective enforcement in terms of a familiar, simple, and unambiguous traffic law, let's return to the three objections to discretionary enforcement with which this section began.

Full Enforcement. First there was the issue of the full-enforcement statutes and their requirement that police enforce all laws. By now you should understand that this requirement is (a) impossible because police do not have the resources to do it; (b) unjust because all law overreaches and criminalizes more than it should, (c) unwise because all just purposes of the law can sometimes be served adequately by not enforcing it; and (d) not to be taken seriously because legislatures know full well as they enact them that a great many laws will not be enforced unless there is active special interest in their enforcement.

Separation of Powers. Second there was the issue of the separation of governmental powers and the argument that selective enforcement usurps the rights of the legislature to make or amend law. By now you should understand that a statement like "We do not say to police, 'Here is a problem. Deal with it.' We say 'Here is a detailed code. Enforce it.'" embodies an abominable misunderstanding of the relationship between the police, the legislative branch of government, and the law. Day in and day out, if police do anything they deal with problems, some of which are more important than others, some of which can be helped by enforcing the law as the legislature wrote it, and others of which cannot. Perhaps the most important implication of the research reported above on the influence of citizen discretion on police selective enforcement practices has to do with this fundamental misconception of the idea of police. Despite the fact that it is fashionable to talk about police as "law enforcement" officers (and police often identify themselves in that way), it should be clear by now that that is neither what they are nor what we expect them to be. The police are not a "law enforcement" agency; they are a "regulatory" agency. They regulate relationships between citizens and between citizens and institutions. What's more, by and large they do so reactively—when someone requests their help because things have gotten out of hand.

A Government of Laws. Third and finally there was the problem of "a government of laws, not men" and the invitations to arbitrariness, favoritism, and discrimination that selective enforcement presents. By now you should realize that "a government of laws, not men" would probably be no better than "a government of men, not laws." The simple fact is that good government requires both. If we cannot write a law specifying that on a certain stretch of road no motorist shall travel in excess of 35 mph without having to rely on a substantial measure of police discretion for its fair enforcement, we should understand that no society—and especially not one as complex as ours—can be governed by mere law.

The problem of arbitrariness, favoritism, and discrimination in selective enforcement is both complicated and controversial. That the cops were "racist pigs" was virtually an axiom of the civil rights protests of the 1960s and early '70s. But although some studies show a possible discriminatory pattern in selective enforcement, the largest and most comprehensive research, performed in some of the nation's largest cities in the middle of the civil rights revolution, does not. Moreover, it does not appear that the discriminatory impact of enforcement would be lessened by making enforcement more strict and less discretionary. A reduction in selective enforcement might well impact more heavily on the poor and people of color, who in this country are disproportionately poorer than whites. As one of the most careful students of the complexities of selective enforcement phrased it:

> There is no reason to believe that the poor drink any more or drive any worse than the well-to-do, but they pick up more than their share of tickets and arrests for such offenses. This is not a matter of discrimination. The poor drive older, more run-down vehicles with more equipment violations, and as a result they will be stopped more often and given more citations for such offenses. [Brown, 1981: 289].

SELECTIVE ENFORCEMENT: THE REAL PROBLEM

I am going to assume that by now you understand that selective enforcement is a just and necessary part of policework and that it cannot be eliminated. I am also going to assume that you understand that police are not a "law enforcement" agency but a "regulatory" agency. Their job, as they practice it, is not to enforce laws but to regulate relationships between people. I am going to assume this much not only because I don't know how to say any more than I have already to convince you of these truths but also because once you accept them it becomes possible to examine the really challenging questions about selective enforcement: What should we do about it? What should be done to improve the quality of selective enforcement decisions? How do we encourage police not to enforce the law when it overreaches, when its legitimate purpose will not be served by making an arrest, when it is a bad law, when to spend time and money enforcing it takes police resources away from more important work, and when social rather than legal forces should be counted on to repair differences between citizens whose relationships police are called upon to regulate? Let's consider three answers to this all important question.

A Mask of Full Enforcement. A common answer to these questions is "Nothing!" Among police who privately concede that the actual work of policing is highly discretionary, there are many who argue that public revelation of the extent of police discretion would undermine their image of impartiality and objectivity and makes policing far more difficult. They point out that a public policy of selective enforcement creates resentment, not only among people who obey the law but also among people who have the law selectively enforced on them. Moreover, when selective enforcement discretion is openly admited and recognized, they claim that it is likely to become a target for special interest groups and open police agencies to unnecessary political pressures of all kinds. Why, advocates of this position ask, open police to these kinds of pressures when there is scant evidence that police have misused or abused their selective enforcement powers? In short, this position amounts to conceding all of what we said above about the necessity and virtue of selective enforcement while arguing that the best thing for police to do about it is to hide it behind a mask of full enforcement, to continue to make believe that it does not exist.

The Public Rulemaking Model. A second answer to the question about what to do about selective enforcement is offered by Kenneth Culp Davis, author of the definition of discretion with which we began this chapter. Recognizing that police are regulatory rather than law enforcement agencies, Davis urges that police begin to behave like other regulatory agencies by making policies that will govern selective enforcement. These policies should guide police officers on the street in making selective enforcement decisions; they should be public; and they should be open to input from interest and activist groups. In fact, Davis suggests that police publicly announce tentative selective enforcement policies and invite interest parties to criticize them and make suggestions before they are put into practice. Making selective enforcement policies public and making them in this public way, Davis argues, will have three primary virtues: (1) Policy will be improved because it will be made in advance by top administrators rather than by individual patrolmen on an ad hoc basis; (2) policy will be improved by being made public because those policies that cannot withstand public scrutiny will be minimized or eliminated; and (3) policy will be improved because, once it is made public, it can be made subject to testing and evaluation and, in response to justifiable criticism, continually modified and refined. In addition, Davis adds, a great benefit of this open process of police rulemaking will be educating the public and the police themselves to the reality that as regulatory agencies, police make vital policy decisions.

The True Professional Model. [6] A third answer to the question of what to do about selective enforcement—an answer we shall call the "true professional model"—concedes a bit to both of the other answers. To the position advocating a mask of full enforcement it concedes that some, but by no means all, police selective enforcement policies must be kept hidden from public scrutiny. Some policies and practices are properly regarded as professional secrets and rightfully deserve to be kept so as a matter of practical necessity. If, for example, police were to announce publicly a selective enforcement policy that said they would not make arrests of persons going less than 10 miles per hour over the posted speed, it is not unreasonable to predict that the overall pace of traffic would pick up to the discretionary limit. Likewise, if police publicly announced a policy of not arresting persons in possession of less than 30 grams of marijuana, the policy is likely to become understood as an endorsement of the practice. Perhaps an even better example of the necessity of a false mask of full enforcement is the practice of the largest regulatory agency in American society, the Internal Revenue Service. The IRS is well aware that a great many people cheat on their income taxes, but they do not have the ability to go after every tax cheat (something almost every tax cheat knows). Effectively, their policy is to allow cheating within certain limits. Of course, it would be absurd for the IRS to announce this as their official policy. As any regulatory agency must do, they publicly announce a "dishonest" policy of full enforcement while practicing secret policies of discretionary selective enforcement. Insofar as the IRS may be said to represent it, a partial mask of full enforcement, dishonest through it may be, is a normal and necessary part of the American democratic regulatory process.

To the advocates of public rulemaking the model of the truly professional police officer concedes the necessity of developing and recognizing selective enforcement policies. However, it parts company with the rulemaking model in three areas. In the one we have just mentioned above, it does so obviously and dramatically. The true professional model holds that a great deal of selective enforcement policy of necessity cannot be made public and some of it may well have to be hidden from public view under a mask of full enforcement.

The second area in which the true professional model differs from the rulemaking model is in the professional model's *primary* reliance on research and professional expertise rather than a process of public policymaking as a way of formulating selective enforcement policy. What the true professional model apspires to do is make a major part of selective enforcement policy not a matter of political debate but a product of technical, scientific knowledge. In many areas research exists or is under way that is directly relevant to selective enforcement policymaking. There is an enormous literature on the deterrent effects of various types of sanctions and the conditions under which they are likely to be effective. Specifically, in the area of traffic enforcement there is good research on the effect that crackdowns on speeders have had on accident rates and traffic safety.[7] We also have convincing research evidence on the effect of increases or decreases in levels of random preventive patrol and police response time on crime rates and the apprehension of criminals.[8] And we can now predict with considerable accuracy whether or not the initial report of a burglary or robbery contains enough information to make it worthwhile spending additional effort to try to solve it.[9] With each of these findings and many others like them a portion of police discretion becomes somewhat less a matter of public debate or police guesswork and somewhat more a matter of technical, professional knowledge.

The third area in which the professional model and the rulemaking model differ is in the amount of selective enforcement discretion each seeks to leave in the hands of individual, street-level officers. Both concede that some selective enforcement discretion must be left at the street level, but the major thrust of the rulemaking model is to find ways to make that discretion a matter over which police administrators may take control. In contrast, the professional model holds that the very nature of policing is such that those individuals who do it must be given broad, discretionary, selective enforcement powers in order to do it properly. In short, the true professional model holds that policing is and ought to be treated as a genuine profession, even though we have never recognized it or treated it as one.

Evaluating the Models

Each of the three models I have outlined above is something more than an answer to the problem of how best to improve the quality of selective enforcement. Each model also embodies a double vision of another kind: a vision, first, of what a good police should be and a vision, second, of the power and authority relationships that ought to exist between the police people whose lives they regulate in a democratic society. Each model embodies both a *moral* and a *political* vision, and any choice among the models is ultimately amoral and political choice as well. I encourage you to draw your own conclusions on the question of which model ought to guide the future of police reform. These models are for *you* to talk about in moral and political terms. What I will try to do for you is identify the issues associated with each model that appear to be most relevant to mature moral and political debate.

The Mask of Full Enforcement. On the face of things the model of a mask of full enforcement would appear to give police more power to control selective enforcement discretion than either of the other two models. However, this appearance may well be more of an illusion than a reality. By denying the existence of selective enforcement discretion, the administration of police agencies is prevented from making the kind of detailed policy that would allow them to take effective control of it. Under a mask of full enforcement some vague understandings of "what the administration wants" may filter down and circulate among officers on the street, but unless officers can be given fairly explicit selective enforcement instructions, they cannot be forced to abide by them. The first political irony of the model of the mask of full enforcement is that although it is worn to prevent undue influence on selective enforcement from politicians, activists, and interest groups outside police agencies, its main impact may be to limit severely internal, administrative, centralized control over the selective enforcement practices of officers on the street.

The second political irony of the model of the mask of full enforcement has to do with the fact that it provides an enormous amount of leverage for influencing police policy to precisely those groups politicians, interest groups, and activists—whom it would at first appear to disenfranchise. Whether it is to request police to protect those who plan to demonstrate for an unpopular case, to register voters of the "wrong" color, to prevent strikers from damaging their employers' property, to prevent employers' thugs from beating up union organizers, to close down vendors of pornographic literature, or to keep open vendors of abortion services, typically what these groups request from police administrators is *more,* not less, police service. The greatest power of police lies not in their capacity to arrest but in their capacity to refuse to arrest. On balance, it may be more important to give citizens the unqualified legal right to demand full enforcement from police than to give police the right to make public selective enforcement policy.

The Public Rulemaking Model. The public rulemaking model seeks to make the creation and administration of selective enforcement policy explicit, public, and centralized. It is often promoted as the most open, honest, and democratic of the three proposals for improving the quality of selective enforcement. This may well be, but it would seem to require a greater increase in police power than either of the other models to achieve the ends of openness, honesty, and democracy.

A substantial increase in the power of top police administrators is a manifest objective of the public rulemaking model. It follows from making selective enforcement policy explicit. By making selective enforcement policy explicit, top police administrators acquire the potential capacity to control how street-level officers exercise selective enforcement discretion. The public rulemaking model is openly a plan to centralize and assume control over the power of selective enforcement discretion, which at present is radically decentralized, controlled largely by individual street-level officers, and influenced most heavily by the preferences of citizen complainants.

The second necessary increase in police power that would seem to be required by the public rulemaking model follows from its aspiration to make selective enforcement policy public. Requiring police to make selective enforcement public will inevitably expose them to political pressures that they must be given sufficient political power to withstand. In some cases this amounts to asking police to take political pressures that legislators themselves refused to take in public. Although many legislators might privately concede no objection to decriminalization of some forms of prostitution, marijuana use, social gambling, or an occasional domestic assault, I suspect that most of those who might would consider it political suicide to take such a stand in public. In politics, as elsewhere, yoghurt flows downhill and under the rug as well.

It is by no means clear where the increase in police political power necessary to take the heat of public selective enforcement policymaking would come from. For the reasons just mentioned, I think it is unlikely to come from legislators or other elected officials. If such power is extended to police, I suspect that it would have to come through making the top administrative positions in police agencies fairly long-term, tenured appointments from which occupants could be removed only by substantial evidence of official misconduct. It is the way we have empowered judges in the federal judicial system to resist the influences of political pressure. De facto, it is the kind of appointment both Richard Mayne and J. Edgar Hoover once enjoyed. Mayne used it to prevent the development of any substantial-sized detective component in the New Police for nearly 40 years. One of the few top executives in the history of American policing to posses sufficient immunity from political pressures to announce openly a wide variety of selective enforcement policies, Hoover used it to keep the FBI from organized crime, narcotics, and white-collar crime investigations for nearly half a century.[10]

Finally, if police administrators gained sufficient power to develop selective enforcement policies in controversial areas, it is by no means clear that they could write them in ways that would improve the quality of street officer decisions. Much of the actual work of enforcing the law or deciding not to enforce it involves acting on an intuitive grasp of the situation and its participants. It may be that this crucial dimension of police discretion cannot be expressed in an administrative policy, any more than a physician's diagnostic or theraputic discretionary judgment can be reduced to the pages of a medical text book.

The True Professional Model. It is hard to find an occupation these days that does not want to be treated as a "profession." The word itself has undergone such an enormous inflation in meaning that virtually everyone whose work requires any kind of discretion at all, from hairdressers to pest exterminators, feel entitled to call themselves professionals. they do so in the hope that title of "professional" will gain them more respect and more money and subject them to less control from their clientele or those who supervise them.

This is exactly what the true professional model wants to get as well. But the model realizes that our society does not willingly give that kind of respect, money, or autonomy lightly. If police are to get to be true professionals— that is, professionals in more than name only—our society allows one and only one path to that status. It must begin with a long period of education in an accredited, academic professional school at the college or postgraduate level, include or continue through a period of supervised internship, and conclude with the granting of a license without which one cannot practice that profession. No true profession—neither medicine nor law, engineering, accounting, teaching, social work, nursing, or clinical psychology—has ever achieved genuine professional status in any other way.

Thirty years ago the prospects for policing to become professionalized in this way appeared very dim. Although there were some calls for college education for police officers as early as the 1930's, as late as 1954 there were no more than 22 college programs in the country that offered any kind of curriculum for police.[11] However, by 1966, following an enormous influx of federal money, the number of programs grew to nearly 200 and by 1975 had climbed to well over 1000.[12] Today, with all of the necessary educational apparatus in place and educational institutions suffering from generally declining enrollments, the prospects for making policing a true profession have never been better. All that is needed is a recognized association to accredit schools to produce licensed police officers and police agencies who are willing, or obliged as a condition for continuing to receive federal or state funding, to begin hiring only graduates of accredited professional schools.

There appear to be two general areas of political controversy over the development of a truly professional police of this kind. The first is that making policing a true profession, which cannot be done without making a college degree a prerequisite, might impede the entry of members of minority groups into police careers. You will remember that policing in the United States has long been used as a path of upward mobility for disadvantaged minorities. The loss of this path may be a cost of the professionalization of police, but I suspect that whether or not it is depends heavily upon the prevailing market for professionals of other kinds. Anyone smart enough to get a college degree should be able to figure out that it is better to be an employed professional police officer than an unemployed professional lawyer.

A second area of profound political concern is with the quality of the college programs themselves. Many of them arose for the sole purpose and with the sole result of taking the money the federal government made available for police education. What they offered police was an illusion of a higher education. What police they enrolled got was an exposure to American higher education's capacities for white-collar crime. Fortunately, the federal money that sustained these programs has now dried up and many of the worst programs have disappeared.

A major controversy still remains, however, over what ought to be taught in a professional police curriculum. Some envision a curriculum similar to that which is offered in schools of engineering: a few core courses in the liberal arts but heavy emphasis on training in the technical and theoretical skills of the discipline. On the other end of the spectrum are those who argue that any technical police training at the undergraduate level is premature specialization. Prospective police should be broadened at the undergraduate level, exposed to new views and different opinions through exposure to arts, literature, languages, philosophy, and the social sciences. Only after such a liberal education should their curriculum be narrowed to the study of the technical aspects of policing.

What makes the curriculum controversy a moral and political issue of relevance to the true professional model is that at its heart is an argument that the whole idea of policing becoming a profession is based on mistaken notion of what the nature of policework is. The argument is that policing is a moral and political occupation, and neither its study nor its practice can be turned into a matter of "technical," "scientific," or "professional" competence. Michael K. Brown makes this argument most elegantly in a criticism of Egon Bittner, the most articulate advocate of reforming police along the lines of the true professional model:

> Though there may be some value in putting police work on a more scientific basis, Bittner's proposal is subject to severe limitations. Bittner is guilty, I believe, of what Max Weber once debunked as "scientism." Unlike most contemporary social scientists Weber had a keen sense of the limits of science, of the questions it could and could not resolve. Science might provide one with factual and even causal knowledge, but it could never answer fundamental questions, those pertaining to what ought to be done. Yet it is precisely such moral issues that are at the core of the problem of discretion, and that a professional knowledge grounded in science cannot answer. The danger, as Weber feared, is that science and technology would encroach on the realm of values and politics and that political decisions would be made on the basis of scientific or pseudoscientific knowledge; or, perhaps worse, such knowledge would be used as a rationalization for decisions [1981: 295].

Brown's criticism, adopted from Weber, is well worth remembering as a warning and a caution to anyone who had occasion to deal with scientists of any stripe, but particularly with social scientists—people like Brown and me.

The response to this most valuable Weberian warning is that although science cannot tell anyone what ought to be done, if someone claims to be doing something, it is one of the best ways we have of finding out whether or not they are actually doing it. This is important because without too much exaggeration it can be said that almost all the major social science research ever conducted on police and policing has shown either that they were not doing what they said they were doing or that they were not achieving the ends they were hoping to achieve. It is probably not possible to build much of a true profession on a foundation of almost uniformly negative findings, but such findings have provoked a number of morally and politically sensitive and sophisticated studies. In the next chapter we shall look at one of the best of them to see what it has to say about good police and good policing.

CONCLUSIONS

Police are a highly discretionary regulatory agency. They exercise discretion in many ways, including choosing when and where and under what conditions to enforce the law. Although selective enforcement of the law is probably illegal in most states, appears to challenge the constitutional doctrine of separation of powers, and places what amounts to an enormous law making power in the hands of individual police officers, it is something we would not want to do without. Because it is a means to an end rather than an end in itself, all law overreaches, has legitimate purposes that may not be well served by enforcing it, and may become bad law when enforced in circumstances to which it was not created to apply. Moreover, because their resources are limited, a limitation legislatures impose and appreciate, police must assign priorities to their enforcement efforts. All of these aspects of selective enforcement make it a necessary and essential feature of good policework.

Despite the fact that policing is and ought to be highly discretionary and police routinely enforce the law very selectively, they are inclined to minimize the importance or deny the existence of discretionary selective enforcement. Partly this is so because full enforcement statutes discourage such disclosures, but hiding behind a mask of full enforcement also makes the day-to-day work of policing easier. If citizens simply assume that all police do is enforce the written law, police do not have to defend their selective enforcement decisions. However, one irony of assuming a mask of full enforcement is that it prevents police administrators from developing detailed selective enforcement policies through which they might be able to assume real control over the selective enforcement decisions line officers make. The other irony is that although a mask of full enforce-

ment may allow police to adopt questionable selective enforcement practices privately, it gives citizens an unqualified legal
right to demand enforcement services. If the real power of
police lies in their discretionary capacity *not* to enforce the
law, this is a substantial right that the elimination of full enforcement statutes and a mask of full enforcement would diminish
or abolish.

To gain administrative control over selective enforcement
practices, to reduce the range of line officer selective enforcement discretion, and to make police selective enforcement policy
open to discussion, debate, and evaluation, a number of students
of police have followed Kenneth Culp Davis's lead in suggesting
that selective enforcement discretion be guided by a public rulemaking model. Under such a model police would announce
proposed selective enforcement policies, invite comment and
criticism, revise proposed policies where police administrators
think the criticism is justified, and put the policies into place
with provisions for their continual evaluation and review. Although
a public rulemaking model would have the effect of educating
the public to how widely discretionary police agencies are, the
chief obstacle to adoption of such a model is the present lack
of police power to stick to a selective enforcement policy in
the face of substantial opposition. In many controversial areas
(e.g., gambling, prostitution, drug use, and domestic violence)
police selective enforcement practices have developed because
legislators have refused to specify under what circumstances
these laws should not be enforced. To require police to make
controversial selective enforcement policies public would
necessitate granting to police administrators political powers
substantially greater than they currently enjoy.

The rationale for increasing the political powers of police
administrators is that the selective enforcement policies they
would develop would substantially increase the quality of selective enforcement decisionmaking of street-level officers. Such
an increase seems doubtful for two reasons. First, the reactive
nature of policing and the great respect police currently show
for the preferences of complainants already structures selective
enforcement in a direction most appropriate in a democratic

Selective Enforcement   119

society. Second, it is not at all clear that administrative selective enforcement policies can prove to be of much help in guiding officers to make sensitive selective enforcement decisions on the street. Those decisions must be made in terms of dimensions of "about-which-something-ought-to-be-done-NOW" situations that can be grasped and evaluated only by the officer on the scene. The true professional model invests most heavily in the individual police officer and on that basis makes its claim as a moral and political guide for the future of American policing. It conceeds that police discretion must be informed by administrative policies, some of which ought to be made public and others of which ought to be kept secret. It central thesis is that police have an enormous power in the discretionary right not to enforce the law that cannot be taken away from them. It cannot be taken by writing more explicit administrative selective enforcement policies any more than we can by writing more explicit laws. In short, it argues that we must trust police and train them to use their power wisely in the same way we must train and trust other professionals in whom we have no choice but to entrust equally impressive powers.

DISCUSSION QUESTIONS

Which model—the mask of full enforcement, the administrative rulemaking model, or the true professional model—is the best moral and political guide for shaping the future of American policing?

NOTES

1. See Kenneth Culp Davis (1969). See also Davis's *Police Discretion* (1975), a less comprehensive work because of its exclusive focus on the problem of selective enforcement.

A very strong competitor in the battle over a proper definition of discretion is offered by Albert J. Reiss, Jr. (1974). Reiss argues that a choice should be regarded as "discretionary" not just because an agency has the power to make it but *only* when it is not, legally or practically, open to review (p. 679).

2. The pioneering article in the recent discovery of the extent of selective enforcement discretion is Joseph Goldstein's "Police Discretion Not to Invoke the Criminal Justice

Process" (1960). The major work emphasizing the breadth of police discretion in areas other than selective enforcement is Herman Goldstein's *Policing A Free Society* (1977).

3. Ronald J. Allen reports in "The Police and Substantive Rulemaking: Reconciling Principle and Expediency" (1976: 71). that 23 states have laws requiring police to arrest anyone who violates any law (Alaska, Arizona, Arkansas, California, Colorado, Connecticut, Delaware, Florida, Idaho, Hawaii, Kentucky, Louisiana, Maryland, Massachusetts, Michigan, Nebraska, New Mexico, North Dakota, Ohio, Utah, Virginia, Washington, and West Virginia); two more have laws requiring that they make arrests in all cases in which a law is violated in there presence (Illinois and Indiana); and two more direct police to arrest all felons (Minnesota and Missouri). We may add to Allen's list a District of Columbia law *D.C. Code Ann.* sec. 414 [Supp. III] 1970) which makes it a crime punishable by two years in prison for a police officer to fail to arrest a person who has committed a crime in his presence.

4. In *Police Discretion* (1975), Davis argues that such laws were never written to be interpreted literally. The Allen article (1976) is the best-known critique of Davis's position.

5. The "proactive"—"reactive" distinction is the conceptual creation of Albert J. Reiss, Jr. in his *Police and the Public* (1971: 64-72). In analysis of 127,861 incidents handled by the patrol division of the Chicago Police between March 31 and April 27, 1966, 93% developed from citizen requests for police service.

6. The model I present in this section is the creation of Egon Bittner who in *The Functions of Police in Modern Society* (1980) outlined it without naming it as a way of making policing a profession. In police circles there is a model of what an ideal police agency should look like called "the professional model." It envisions a police agency organized along military lines, highly centralized, strictly disciplined, exceptionally efficient, technologically sophisticated, free from the influence of partisan politics, and staffed by officers of honor and integrity. An instrument of reform in the history of American policing, the objective of the police professional model is to establish a high degree of command control over the work of policemen. This is almost exactly the opposite of the goal of the Bittner model, and I have called Bittner's model "the true professional model" in hopes of reducing confusion that might result from the similarity in names.

7. See John A. Gardiner (1969). On the basis of enforcement statistics from nearly 700 police departments and detailed case studies of enforcement in four American cities, as well as detailed review of available literature from this country and abroad, Gardiner concludes that

> it is possible that accidents rates might go up if the police adopted a publicly known policy of complete nonenforcement of traffic laws, or go down if drastic penalties were instituted (such as mandatory suspensions for speeding or the Bulgarian policy of a death sentence for a second conviction for drunken driving). But no evidence was found to support the theory that high ticketing will produce a low accident rate [p.162].

8. See George Kelling et al. (1974) and Spelman and Brown (1983: 160-168). I have summarized the major findings of each study as follows:

> It makes about as much sense to have police patrol routinely in police cars to fight fire as it does to have firemen patrol routinely in fire trucks to fight fire.

Police currently make on-scene arrests in about 3 percent of the serious crimes reported to them. If they traveled faster than a speeding bullet to the reports of all serious crimes, this on-scene arrest rate would rise no higher than 5 percent (p. 130).

9. See Bernard Greenberg et al. (1972). What Greenberg found was that the vast majority of burglary and robbery complaints detectives were routinely assigned to follow up after patrolmen had taken the initial reports had virtually no chance of being solved.

10. There are many books on J. Edgar Hoover and the FBI, but Sanford J. Unger's *FBI* (1976) remains the most balanced and most comprehensive study, although a highly critical work by A. G. Theoharris, *Spying on Americans* (1978) is essential reading for anyone interested in the history of the agency.

11. This pioneering effort to recruit college-educated police officers was the work of August Vollmer, one of the great figures in the history of American policing. See Nathan Douthit (1975). Vollmer's effort to recruit college-educated police was helped in no small measure by the Great Depression, which made it difficult for them to find what would have been regarded as respectable work for college graduates.

12. These figures on the number of college programs are reported in Herman Goldstein (1977: 285).

6

GOOD POLICE AND GOOD POLICING

What makes a good police officer? What type of organizational, political, and social environment encourages good policework? In this chapter I am going to explore one very sophisticated answer to these two questions. It is the answer given by William Ker Muir in a book entitled *Police: Streetcorner Politicians* (1977). Muir developed it in the course of an observation study of 28 policemen in an unnamed American city, but ultimately it is based on a bold and far-reaching theory, only small parts of which have been subjected to test. Nevertheless, I know of no other treatment of either of these questions that can be of more help in moving you to a mature and responsible understanding of the issues that must considered before answering them. For this reason, Muir's theory is a good place to end this beginning book on police because it takes you to the very frontiers of what we think we know about them.

MUIR'S THEORY

It is probably best to think of Muir's general theory as having three parts. The first is an analysis of the nature of coercive power and the special problems faced by people who assume the responsiblity of coercing others. The second is an analysis of how coercive power affects personality and how personality affects the way different types of people respond to the challenges and responsibilities of using coercive means. The third part of Muir's general theory is an analysis of conditions that discourage excessive use of coercive means and encourage police officers to develop in morally and politically mature ways. Let's begin with the first part of Muir's theory, his analysis of the nature of coercive power.

The Nature of Coercive Power

To appreciate the nature of coercive power Muir creates a special kind of device with which to think about it: a *model*. Muir's model, which he calls "the extortionate transaction," is an abstract representation of coercive relationships of any kind. Muir's model may refer to legally legitimate coercion by police officers; illegal coercion by kidnappers, blackmailers, and other criminal extortionists; domestic coercion between spouses or between parents and children; or even coercion nations practice against one another when they threaten war, invasion, or economic sanctions. Whether good or bad, moral or immoral, legal or illegal, all of these relationships fit Muir's model of the extortionate transaction because one party in the relationship tries to control the behavior of the others through threats to hurt them or things they care about.

The really important feature of Muri's model is not that it applys to legitimate as well as illegitimate transactions, but that it is the *simplest possible model* of a coercive relationship. Muir's model contains only five terms: a *victim,* a *victimizer,* a *hostage,* a *ransom,* and a *threat.* In fact, Muir's model of the extortionate transaction is so simple that it can be fully summarized in just one sentence: The extortionate transaction may be said to exist whenever a *"threat* is made by the *victimizer* committing him to injure the *hostage* (something the victim values very much) unless the *victim* will pay a *ransom* (something he prefers to give up to save the *hostage* from harm.)" (1977:38). Although we normally think of a "hostage" as a person and of "ransom" as a sum of money, you will note that in Muir's model neither of these terms is limited in this way. A "hostage" can be anything a victim values very much: not only a person but also a possession, the victim's social standing or reputation, the victim's life or physical well-being. The same is true of the idea of "ransom": Ransom may refer to a sum of money, but it can also refer to an object or an act or a type of behavior the victimizer wishes to coerce from the victim.

In terms of Muir's model, if a police officer yells to a fleeing felon "Stop or I'll shoot!" and the felon stops, the officer (the victimizer) has extorted the "ransom" of getting the felon to stop by threatening to harm the "hostage" of the felon's (the victim's) life.

If Muir's model of the extortionate transaction is that simple, what makes it so powerful and such a useful tool for thinking through the complexities of coercive relations? How can it help us understand how to coerce effectively or to avoid being coerced? The secret of its power is its simplicity. Because a coercive relationship cannot exist if any one of the five terms in Muir's model is eliminated, the model can show us how to avoid being coerced. To do so, all one has to do is eliminate any one of its essential elements. Likewise, because it identifies the essential components necessary to create and sustain a coercive relationship, it has the capacity to teach us what to do to coerce effectively. All of this is quite abstract, but it should become clearer as we show how Muir manipulates his model to develop what he calls the four "paradoxes of coercive power" and how each of these paradoxes bears on the coercive capacities of police.

The Paradox of Dispossession: "The less one has, the less one has to lose." One of the lessons of Muir's model has to do with the essential role of the *hostage*. Without something to take hostage, a coercive relationship cannot exist. In order to coerce a person the potential victim must have something that a victimizer can take hostage. If not, coercion is impossible. Likewise, if a victim has a great many possessions that may be taken hostage, coercion of that kind of person is likely to be easy. How do these two general principles, both of which derive directly from Muir's model, help us to understand the special features of the coercive role of the police?

One important implication has to do with whom the police are most capable of coercing and what the police are most likely to threaten to take hostage in order to police them. Souls like you and me (more or less middle class, college educated or trying to be, and relatively well-off) are virtually dripping with things police can threaten to take hostage. Our careers and reputations would be severely damaged by a public confrontation with police. An arrest, even if the charges were subsequently dropped, would cause us embarrassment and humiliation. We pay traffic fines and parking tickets not just because our legal right to drive, on which our social and occupational lives depend, is held hostage against us, but also because our valuable time and important commitments are held hostage by the threat of someday finding our car immobilized by a police "boot." So, despite the fact that our possessions, resources, friendships, occupation, reputation, and position in the community appear to give us power to resist being coerced, they actually have the opposite effect. This is what makes the paradox of dispossession a paradox: All of our valuable possessions, all the things we have that might appear to put us in a position of strength in a coercive encounter, actually make us weaker. We have so much to lose in a coercive encounter, so much that can be taken hostage and hurt, and so much that we can well afford to give up in ransom that we are fools if we fail to pay police the ransom of compliance with their orders.

Things are, as you may have already guessed, different when it comes to policing people who are radically different from us: life's real losers, persons without jobs or property or reputation or social standing or any other material or social possessions police can threaten to take hostage in order to coerce them. Short of actually laying hands on such unfortunate people and physically forcing them to do something, how can they be coerced? To coerce the truly dispossessed, police are inclined to threaten to injure the only hostages that such unfortunate people offer: their freedom, such as it is, and their bodies.

There is, however, one other option: to try to find some way of "re-possessing" the dispossessed, of giving them things of value so that those things, rather than their freedom and their bodies, can be taken hostage. Expressed in such an abstract way, this sounds like a terribly cold and calculating strategy, but it need not be. Muir offers as an example of this kind of strategy the policework of an officer he calls Mike Marshall. Marshall's beat is "skid row," an area inhabited by more than its share of the truly dispossessed. The secret of Marshall's success in policing the truly dispossessed is that Marshall works his beat and develops a reputation among the inhabitants of skid row as an officer they can trust and from whom they can receive help, understanding, and decent treatment. He is a counselor to "his bums," as he calls them, knows almost all of them by name, and serves as their social worker, legal advisor, and dispute mediator. He is even their loan office at times, dispensing from his own pocket a quarter or half a dollar and understanding that it may be quite a while before the loan is repaid. By working his beat in this way Marshall has become an institution on skid row. But more important, he has given the dispossessed of skid row a valuable possession they do not want to lose—Marshall himself. Hence, more often than not Marshall can rely on those people he has helped and others who know of the good work he has done on skid row to come to his aid when he requires their assistance.

The Paradox of Detachment: "The less the victim cares about preserving something, the less the victimizer cares about taking it hostage." The second paradox Muir derives from his simple model of the extortionate transaction also has to do with the element of the hostage. But unlike the paradox of dispossession, which had to do with the sheer number of things people possess that can be taken hostage, the paradox of detachment has to do with the importance or the value of those things to the people who have them. It is possible to conceive of a person with a great many possessions who doesn't care at all about losing any of them. If that's the case, then it will be impossible to coerce that person by threatening to take or harm those possessions.

This second paradox of coercive power is important to understanding the work of policing because police frequently confront situations in which people have become detached from things they would normally value and behave as if those things meant nothing to them. An example is what Muir calls "the family beef." In it the police officer typically finds a husband and wife who have become detached from all that was once important to them. They are fighting, throwing things, smashing the possessions they once worked to accumulate, damaging whatever investments they have made in a neighborhood reputation for respectability and propriety, hurting each other, and, in turn, themselves. Under such conditions, detached from the value of everything, the couple in the throes of the family beef offer the police officer almost nothing to take hostage in order to coerce from them the ransom of control. It should come as no surprise that the family beef is one of the most dangerous situations a police officer can confront.

One way to police such situations is to use coercive force on one or both of the spouses and take one of them, at least temporarily, into custody. But as was true with the paradox of dispossession, the model of the extortionate transaction suggests an alternative strategy. The officer can attempt to "re-attach" the spouses to the value of at least some of those things from which they have become detached. In describing the strategy of one officer, Joe Wilkes, whom Muir observed to work family beefs in this way, Muir emphasizes that the crucial element is the officer's ability to find something that had once been important to the couple and to talk to them about it in a way that will re-attach them to the value it once had and the hope it represents for the future.

> So, in a family beef, Joe Wilkes talked. "My own personality is to talk," he said. He articulated a perspective of hope for the husband and wife: "We talk about his possibilities—about everything he had possibilities for." To touch men's hopes, he sought to detect old attachments that had made the past meaningful—to scent out the "glue" that had held together their center.... He looked for anything that had once been important to the marriage—a car that was well taken care of, a valuable domino set, a good-smelling pot of soup on the stove, a spotless kitchen—anything which had been beloved, any basis for hopefullness.... [H]e simply tried to remind his citizenry of their traditions, of who they were, of what had been meaningful to them—and to assure them that it had been worthwhile thus far and was still worthwhile persevering for. He worked on their hopes. [Muir, 1977:98-99].

The Paradox of Irrationality: "The more delirious the threatener, the more serious the threat: the more delirious the victim, the less serious the threat." The third paradox of coercive power that Muir derives from his model of the extortionate transaction has to do with the element of the threat, the capacity of the victim to appreciate it, and the willingness of the victimizer to carry it out. This paradox bears on police and policing in a very special way.

It dramatizes the difficulty of coercing those who are unwilling or unable to understand that a hostage they value is being threatened. Many people the police routinely encounter are in mental states (e.g., drunk, crazy, high, terrorized, traumatized, or insane with anger) that make them virtually immune to coercive threats. It is frequently the job of police to control people in such irrational mental states, but the extortionate transaction teaches us that if they are so irrational they cannot comprehend a threat, short of actually using coercive force, they cannot be coerced.

But as was true with the first two paradoxes of coercive power, the model of the extortionate transaction also suggests an alternative to using coercive force when trying to coerce people who are irrational. The alternative, as you probably have already guessed, is to try to find some way to restore them to rationality, to a state of realistic fearfulness. In some situations the person the police are trying to coerce may be too far gone to admit this kind of strategy, but in others police can employ devices that serve to move irrational persons into states of increasing rationality. Sometimes, as in confrontations with people who are only momentarily confused or terrified, this work of bringing a person back to rationality can be accomplished with little more than a calm, confident, understanding, and reassuring voice. At other times, more elaborate and less gentle strategies may be necessary.

Muir's example of good policing in the face of the paradox of irrationality is the work of an officer he calls Bill Douglas. A major problem Douglas deals with on his beat are large numbers of juveniles who are truant from school, congregate in places where they are unwelcome, and disturb the peace. The juveniles, junior high and high school students, may be described as irrational because they simply do not understand the consequences of their behavior. They are oblivious to the effect their truancy will have on their chances of going on to college, or, worse still, they don't even care. They do not appreciate the effect they are having on the neighborhood they frequent, the business they drive away from local stores, or their effect on pedestrians who are frightened or intimidated by gangs of rowdy, truant youths. Most of all, they have no sense of what an arrest for truancy or disturbing the peace or drinking or drugs might do to their future or the costs it could involve in time and legal fees, in personal embarassment, in loss of reputation, or in public humiliation of their parents. In short, the teenage truants on Douglas's beat were so preoccupied by their juvenile capers that it rendered them irrationally irresponsible and unafraid of what the real harm the law could visit upon them. Douglas once remarked to Muir, "I'd rather chase burglars or robbers because they're scared of us."

Douglas's job was to restore that rational fear of the real harms that could befall the juveniles without actually causing them to suffer all those harms and all the damaging consequences. He employed a number of inventive strategies to that end. First, he made it his business to learn the name, address, and background of every truant juvenile he found on his beat. Painstakingly and in full view of the juvenile he stopped, Douglas recorded this information in a notebook he always carried with him. This act robbed the juvenile of the anonymity that being in a crowd gave him. At the same time it let him know that Douglas had the capacity to single him out of a crowd or to find him if Douglas saw him running from the scene of a disturbance.

Second, after stopping the juvenile and taking down the information that allowed Douglas to make this particular juvenile the object of future attention, Douglas explained in no uncertain terms what he expected from this juvenile in the future. Douglas made it clear that the next time the youth got into trouble, was found on the streets during school hours or loitering on a corner where he was not welcome, the youth would be arrested. Normally, however, Douglas would extend to the juveniles on his beat one second chance, but only one. If he found a juvenile truant or disorderly a second time, the youth's offense would get conspicuously recorded in Douglas's ever-present notebook and Douglas would emphasize that that youth sh~··'~ expect no further leniency. Any further problem would land the youth in jail.

Third, although Douglas was tolerant in this way, he was not "Officer Friendly" or "Mr. Nice Guy." He knew that the juveniles on his beat would read that type of behavior as weakness and fail to respect him. He used humor in dealing with the youths on his beat, but he wanted them to see him as an officer who was tough and unflinching, someone they could not deceive, someone who knew what they were really up to, someone they could not "bullshit'" with a phoney story or a lame excuse. What Douglas's methods allowed him to develop in the irrational juveniles on his beat was a slowly progressive fear of what they were doing to themselves and what Douglas could and would do to them if they continued along the path of irresponsible and irrational behavior they had been following. Once this rational fear taught the juveniles on Douglas's beat this much, Douglas gained the power to coerce them.

We should not let the paradox of irrationality pass without noting at least one additional implication of it for police. If police wish to increase their power to coerce rational persons, the paradox of irrationality advises them to appear irrational in their willingness to carry through whatever threats they make. In the paradoxical world of coercive encounters, the police officer who is crazy enough to go any length to carry out a threat (e.g., who is willing to shoot to kill a motorist who refuses to move his car from a no-parking zone) is a police officer any rational person will obey!

The Paradox of Face: "The nastier one's reputation, the less nasty one has to be." The paradox of irrationality advised police that if they wish to increase their coercive power, they must appear irrational in their willingness to carry through on their threats. The fourth and final paradox of coercive power, the paradox of face, goes even further. It advises police who wish to increase their coercive capacities to develop a reputation for nastiness, for cruel and brutal treatment of those they threaten.

This advice issues from the model of the extortionate transaction because the element of threat in that model is essentially psychological. What is important about the threat in any extortionate transaction is that the victim must believe that the victimizer will carry through on it. Therefore, it follows that the more nasty, cruel, and brutal the reputation of the victimizer, the more likely the victim will be inclined to believe the victimizer's threat. If a victimizer's reputation is sufficiently nasty, the victimizer may never have to carry through on a threat. If we wish to reduce the actual use of coercive force by police, the paradox of face teaches us that one way to do so is to get them to develop a fearsome reputation for their willingness to use it.

There are, however, three major problems with the advice that issues from the paradox of face. All of them apply equally well to the recommendation of the paradox of irrationality that police create a reputation for irrational willingness to carry through on their threats. The first problem is that if police reputations for nastiness and craziness are to be created, maintained, and continue to prove useful in coercive intimidation, their reputations for irrationality and vindictiveness must be based on some real and repeated acts of genuine irrationality and extreme violence. In a democratic society, we would probably be unwilling to permit police to commit such atrocious and bizarre acts, even if it could be shown that by allowing them to do so we would ultimately reduce the overall amount of coercive force they would be obliged to use.

The second and related problem has to do with the capacity of citizens to respond in kind to a police reputation for craziness and nastiness. The fact is that even if we were very generous in allowing our police to engage in acts that would create and sustain reputations for irrationality and willingness to use violence, the capacity of citizens to respond to those acts with even more irrationality and more extensive violence is, in any democratic society, infinitely greater. The extortionate transaction is, after all, the perfect example of the "vicious cycle." A crazy or nasty threat by one party invites an even crazier and more extreme threat in return. In such an exchange the genuine sadist, the true madman, zealous political terrorist, or the riotous mob always has the upper hand.

A third problem has to do with the effect a police reputation for craziness and nastiness would be likely to have on the type of policing Mike Marshall does on skid row, Joe Wilkes does in the family beef, and Bill Douglas does with the truant juveniles on his beat. A police reputation for craziness and cruelty would serve to undermine the restrained strategies and styles of those excellent officers.

Police Personality and the Nature of Coercive Power

Muir's model of the extortionate transaction and the four paradoxes of coercive power that it yields present police with a range of choices about how they should respond to the challenges of exercising coercive power. Some of them lead to a crude, violent, insensitive, and cruel style of policing: others stand out as choices that lead to good relations with citizens and minimize the actual use of coercive force. The next step Muir takes in building his theory is to determine why some police officers—officers like Marshall, Wilkes, and Douglas—adopt the skilled, humane, and effective policing styles that they do, whereas other officers are either unable to police effectively or do so in unncessarily crude and violent ways.

To probe this question about the relationship between police personality and coercive power, Muir employs another model. Unlike the model of the extortionate transaction that is Muir's own creation, the model he uses to sort out the relationship between police personality and coercive power was created by someone else. It is called the "professional political model" and it was originally proposed by the great German sociologist, Max Weber. In order to appreciate what Weber's model is and what it seeks to do, it will be helpful if you understand just a little bit about the circumstances surrounding its creation.

"Politics as a Vocation"

Weber first described the professional political model in a speech entitled "Politics as a Vocation" (1946). In 1918 Weber gave the speech at the University of Munich to an audience composed largely of advanced students of law and political science. Weber knew that many of the young students in his audience would go on to careers in politics. The task he took up in his speech to these young students was to warn them of the very grave, very real, and very special moral dangers they would inevitably have to face if they took up a career in politics.

As Weber saw it, at the core of every politician's professional life is a genuine moral dilemma. The source of the dilemma is an irreconcilable tension between means and ends. To state it in its simplest terms, the dilemma is that every politician must, on some occasion use morally dirty means in order to achieve morally good ends. What makes the politician's situation a genuine moral dilemma, a situation from which it is impossible to escape without committing a moral wrong, is that if politicians do employ those dirty means, they become morally guilty for having done so. On the other hand, if they fail to employ those dirty means, they become morally guilty of failing to achieve the good ends that can be achieved only by using those dirty means. The type of dirty means Weber had in mind were lies and threats, hurting or threatening to hurt people or the things they valued dearly, behaving irrationally and without care for what any normal person would treasure, and committing or causing to be committed acts of violence and brutality. For reasons you can now appreciate from having studied Muir's model of the extortionate transaction, all of these acts were sometimes required of politicians because they assumed the responsibility of exercising coercive power. These dirty acts are, of course, the obligations imposed on powerful people by the paradoxes of dispossession, detachment, irrationality, and face.

Try to imagine the impact that this presentation by Weber had on the audience of students he faced in Munich in 1918. Here were young students who were undoubtedly committed to ideals of doing good, of helping people, of promoting justice, of preserving freedom, and of achieving peace and decency. Moreover, they were undoubtedly looking forward to doing these things in honest and decent ways, of preserving their own self-respect, of being proud of what they had done in their careers in public service. What Weber told them was that they could not have it both ways. Either they would fail to achieve the good and just ends they so hoped to achieve or they would be forced to resort to morally dirty and shameful means to achieve them. One way or another the responsibility of exercising coercive power would inevitably corrupt them and there was no way to avoid it.

To the students he had now told would be corrupted by the choice of a career in politics, Weber proposed four alternatives. One was that they could give up the idea of a political career. If they were unwilling to be corrupted by the morally devastating responsibilities of exercising coercive power, they had no business becoming politicians. Second, they could abandon their passionate hopes for using their power to achieve the great ideals of doing good, helping people, promoting justice, preserving freedom, and achieving peace and decency and reconcile themselves to careers as obedient bureaucrats. In this role they could play by the rules and their souls would not be endangered by having to resort to dirty means. They would, however, fail at achieving the good ends they once hoped to achieve. Third, they could hold on to their passionate ideals but abandon their respect for civilized means for achieving them. They could learn to lie, deceive, extort, hurt, harm, kill, or injure without suffering guilt or moral reservation. Understandably, none of these three alternatives appealed to Weber's audience anymore than they appeal to us as models of the kind of politicians we want to govern us.

The fourth alternative proposed by Weber was what he called the model of the "mature man." It is what Muir calls Weber's professional political model. As Weber presented it, the problem of the professional politician was to suffer the morally devastating pressures of exercising coercive power without crumbling, without abandoning his ideals, and without becoming bitter and cynical. To achieve this the "mature man" or "professional politician" had to develop and cultivate two virtues. One was moral, the other intellectual. The moral virtue Weber called "passion." It is the strong conviction that the achievement of certain just ends are so important that it allows the mature man to reconcile himself to using morally dangerous, coercive, or violent means to achieve them. The politician who cannot integrate violence into ethics has no place in politics.

The second virtue Weber required of the mature man or professional politician was the intellectual virtue of "perspective." It served as a counterbalance to passion. What Weber meant by it was an ability to see what we sometimes call "the big picture." Perspective put professional politicians' passions into relations with the passions and perspectives of others. It kept them mindful that they and their passions were but one part of a rich and complex world which it was their professional responsibility to work to understand. Most of all it caused them to respect the suffering, the sorrows, the pain, and the sensitivities of others. Perspective taught the professional politician tragedy and tragedy taught the professional politician limits.

Passion and perspective worked to discourage the most damaging effects of the responsibility of exercising coercive power. Passion kept professional politicians from retreating from responsibilities, either by giving up their political careers or settling in to a bureaucratic mentality of blindly doing one's assigned job according to conventional rules. Perspective checked the professional politicians' tendencies to resort to using dirty means too quickly. It did not prevent them from using them altogether, but it restrained them in their use and prevented them from becoming insensitive to the pain and suffering their use of dirty means imposed on others. It is important to emphasize that Weber's model of the mature man or professional politician did not relieve the person who took up the responsibility of exercizing coercive powers from the moral corruption that came with that responsibility. All that Weber's model offered to the young would-be politicians who sat before him in Munich in 1918 was a way of suffering that corruption so they could bear up under its strains and continue to meet the demands of exercizing coercive power.

Muir's Typology

It is Muir's great contribution to see to be true of police and policing what Weber saw to be true for politicians. Both are instances of powerful persons whose careers will be shaped by how they work through the moral and intellectual demands of exercising coercive power. Whether a police officer surrenders his professional responsibilities to a blank bureaucratic role, retreats completely by quitting or avoiding work, becomes a fearsome and ruthless bully, or works to develop a restrained but passionate professional policing style depends upon the extent to which he manages to develop moral passion and a tragic perspective.

Muir expresses this interplay between passion and perspective in police personalities in a systematic way. The interrelationships are relatively easy to understand if you refer to Figure 6.1. What it displays are four possible relationships between passion and perspective, each of which describes a different type of police personality. In box A there is the "professional" who possesses both passion and perspective. In box B we find a type of officer Muir calls the "reciprocator." He has perspective but lacks passion. In box C we find the "enforcer," who is passionate but lacks perspective. Finally, in box D is the "avoider," the officer without passion or perspective, the empty cop who neither cares about nor understands what policework demands.

In order to help you get a feel for exactly how the moral virtue of passion and the intellectual virtue of perspective interplay in each of Muir's four types of police personality, it would be most helpful if you and I both knew intimately some officers who corresponded to each type. Unfortunately, this is not the case. Moreover, in this little book I cannot take the time or the space to describe in sufficient depth the personalities of officers I know who nicely illustrate Muir's types. The problem is that unless I can make reference to some common characters within which passion and perspective can be seen to be at work in living ways, anything I say about passion, perspective, and their effects on police personality is likely to be sterile.

To solve this problem what I am going to do is describe passion and perspective as I find them in some fictional police officers with whom I hope you are familiar: Mick Belker, Howard Hunter, Henry Goldblume, Andy Renko, and Lucy Bates. Since 1980 they have policed the Hill Street District of an unnamed city on a weekly basis and earned 25 Emmeys for doing such

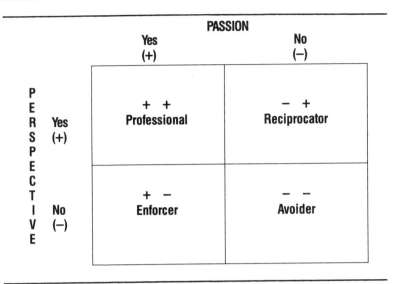

Figure 6.1 Passion, Perspective, and Police Personality

an exemplary job at it. If you do not know them, read on anyway. I will try to say enough about each of them to allow you to follow along. If you do know them, I am sure I can teach you to see them in some new ways. Admittedly, they are not real characters, but each character is real enough for our purposes.

Passion without Perspective: The Enforcers, Mick Belker and Howard Hunter. If any two officers on Hill Street can be said to be morally comfortable with violence and coercion, it is Mick Belker and Howard Hunter. Belker's passion is so near the surface of his personality that even when he is mildly provoked he breaks into an animal-like growl. In coercive encounters he is nothing less than an explosion of violence. Belker bites and kicks and snarls and fights with absolutely mad abandon. Grubby, dirty, dispossessed, and detached from the value of everything (except his mother, who is kept safely fortified and out of sight), Belker offers nothing for a potential victimizer to take hostage. He professes to be willing to rip your lungs out and eat them for lunch, and you would be wise to take his threats seriously. It is hard to imagine how all of the terrifying advice of the four paradoxes of coercive power could be more tightly bundled in one man.

In his personal habits and style Lt. Howard Hunter, leader of the EATers (the Emergency Action Team, Hill Street's paramilitary SWAT squad), is the polar opposite of Mick Belker. Impeccably dressed in dashing military attire and mannerly to a fault, Howard is a perfect officer and gentleman. His job is to use violence, and he is completely comfortable with the morality of his work. He employs violence with clinical coolness and precision. Expert with the tools that magnify destructive forces, he is an unequivocal advocate of their capacity to eliminate problems quickly and efficiently.

Although Belker and Howard are equally comfortable with the morality of violence, it might appear that these two men who are so radically different in police style and personal demeanor could have nothing else in common. Despite appearances, with respect to what Weber and Muir would have us understand as "perspective" both men are virtually identical. For both humankind is divisible into two warring camps. On one side are those who are good and on the other, those who are evil. The only difference in their world view is a matter of rhetoric. Where Howard would find "the beleaguered citizenry of a free-enterprise republic, shoulder to the wheel and nose to the grindstone, gamely carrying on the noble spirit of a thousand years of Anglo-Saxon cerebral and cultural superiority" Belker finds "good people." Where Howard would find "the residue of imprudent breeding bleating at the trough of the welfare state," Belker finds "punks," "hairballs," "maggots," and "dog drool."

Is is precisely because the intellectual perspective of both men is formed in this way that allows each of them to become so comfortable with violence. As long as each can envision the victims of his violence as being of a different and inferior order of life, moral reconciliation with inflicting violence on them in the name of all that's good and decent becomes very easy. In the war on crime Howard is a commanding officer, Belker is a guerrilla fighter.

The problem with this moral reconciliation is that both men purchase it at the cost of gross distortion of the world in which they work. Each entertains a black-and-white, good guys/bad guys, "Us"/"Them" view of the world that is just plain wrong. The world is simply not that simple, and in some of the most touching episodes of *Hill Street Blues* Belker and Howard almost find that out. In one such episode Howard attempts suicide when he becomes unable to cope with the disclosure of his role in a corruption scheme. Although the incident happened many years ago when Howard was a mere rookie, if the world is truly divided into those who are good and those who are evil, the incontrovertible evidence of his own crime left Howard no other option but to see himself as one of "Them." Fortunately, Howard's suicide attempt failed. Since then he has been seeing a psychiatrist.

Belker's intellectual perspective is shaken every time he confronts some dog-droll maggot whom Belker discovers is a lot like him. This is the most fundamental point of what Weber and Muir mean by perspective—the ability to see a common humanity in all people and to appreciate their sorrows and their suffering no matter how different from you they first appear. In two brilliant episodes Belker struggles against this truth as it is taught to him by two improbable teachers: "Captain Freedom," a truly crazy, Batman-caped crime fighter whose passion and perspective is a parody of Belker's, and a wheelchair-bound vandal who first got on Belker's good side by accusing him of not having enough guts to pull off an undercover role as a cripple.

Perspective without Passion: The Reciprocator, Henry Goldblume. If anyone on Hill Street has what Weber and Muir mean by perspective, it is Lt. Henry Goldblume. No one on the Hill is more sensitive to the suffering of the poor, the fears of the weak, or the pains of those who bear the anger of ignorance, injustice, and discrimination. Henry's specialty is hostage negotiation. It is a role for which he is perfectly suited. It requires him to do three things he absolutely believes in—to understand, exchange, and persuade—in order to avoid one thing he categorically abhors—violence. When a hostage, or a hostage-taker, is hurt, a bit of Henry is hurt too. Not an ounce of macho in him, Henry is Hill Street's perfectly liberated male, just as Howard is Hill Street's perfect military gentleman.

In an episode that aired early in the fall of 1984, Henry's former wife was raped. She refused to file a complaint because she did not want to suffer the humiliation of a trial. Without her knowledge, Henry conducted an investigation and identified her rapist. Although his former wife was still unwilling to press charges, Henry confronted the man in a situation in which he could have killed him and escaped prosecution. Although he was sorely tempted, his respect for law and life prevented him from doing so. Later that day he returned to his former wife to urge her to reconsider her decision not to prosecute. Shaken by his nearly having killed another human being, Henry told her about what he had almost done. Henry expected sympathy from her for the emotional trauma he had just been through, as well as some respect for his restraint. Instead, she was disgusted with him for not being man enough to kill the "animal" who had raped her.

Henry lacks passion. This is not to say that he does not care deeply and with all his heart about many things. He does, and he is nothing less than morally courageous in defending his belief in them. But as Weber and Muir use the term, "passion" means something else. Defined in this special way, "passion" means only the ability to reconcile oneself morally to using violent means to achieve the just ends. That is something Henry is morally unable to do.

What you must try to appreciate is why Henry is incapable of doing so. Unlike Howard and Belker, whose worlds are more or less neatly divided into good and evil, black and white, "Us" and "Them," Henry's great virtue is that he sees a unitary conception of all humankind. From Henry's perspective there are no good or evil people, not black and white but shifting shades of gray, no Us and Them, just "We." For obvious reasons this perspective makes his moral reconciliation with coercion much more difficult than it is for Howard and Belker. But Henry adds to it another insight that makes it virtually impossible. His sympathy for the poor, the weak, the culturally deprived, and the socially and mentally handicapped causes Henry to see them exclusively as victims of disabling forces. In Henry's view the tragic lives of these sad souls are not of their own doing. They lack free will. Hence it is the forces of injustice, inequality, and discrimination that need correction and not their poor, weak, troubled, or understandably angry products. In short, they have been victimized enough. Henry cannot bring himself to victimize them further.

Passion and Perspective: The Professionals, Andy Renko and Lucy Bates. Before we look at passion and perspective in Andy Renko and Lucy Bates, let's quickly note two ways in which both are very different from Howard, Belker, and Henry. First, both of them work uniformed assignments. Occasionally each is called upon to play a specialized police role, to work a stakeout or an undercover operation, but by and large they work patrol. This makes them part of a social group of police equals with whom they socialize easily both on and off the job. Howard, Belker, and Henry are not only specialists, but all of them have temperaments and interests that separate them from the social life of patrol. Although he encourages *esprit de corps,* Howard keeps his EATers at military distance. Henry has no sense of humor, is not socially outgoing, and has little interest in sports, drinking, gambling, or nonmeaningful relationships, the stuff of which the locker-room culture of police patrol squads often appears preoccupied. If Belker's nastiness were not sufficient to isolate him socially, his bad breath and body odor would serve the purpose.

Second, both Lucy and Renko have partners with whom they work side by side, eight hours a day, five days a week. Lucy has Joe Coffey, a handsome, decent, but still slightly shallow young jock who grows a little deeper as he and Lucy gain experience together. Renko partners with Bobby Hill, a steady and reserved black man whose tolerance and patience with Renko's emotional excesses is repaid by the entertainment of his company. For both Lucy and Renko these partnerships provide them with a special kind of sanctuary within which they can freely and frankly discuss what they see and how they feel without fear of ridicule or exposure. It is a sanctuary for intimate talk, for exploring emotions and ideas, for moral and intellectual experimentation with a companion who has shared the same experiences. It is a sanctuary Howard, Belker, and Harold, without partners, do not enjoy.

The social security of their patrol squad and the intimate sanctuary of their partnerships provide Lucy and Renko with the environment they need to work through a balance between passion and perspective. It is clear that Lucy had perspective before she ever put on a police uniform. She brought it with her from her background. At least some of it came from the kind of lessons and expectations our society still teaches women—to be sensitive and caring, to feel for those who are poor, weak, troubled, or otherwise less fortunate. But other parts of Lucy's perspective surely come from bucking the traditionally accepted woman's role. In her youth she probably was a tomboy. Although I don't recall it ever being stated on the show (I confess to having missed some episodes), I'll wager that she was brought up in a family of brothers. She was good enough to make a starting slot on the basketball team Hill Street assembled to play against a group of local gang youths. No one—and especially not a woman—would be chosen to represent Hill Street in the annual, citywide, high-stakes, intradepartmental poker game who was not already saavy to that cigar-chomping card world. These experiences and others like them viewers have not yet seen deepen Lucy's perspective. Through them she has challenged the very notion that others are fundamentally different from herself.

As a police officer Lucy's problems were with passion. As is true for most police officers at some time early in their careers, they must demonstrate to other officers and especially their partners that they can be depended upon when the going gets tough. Lucy had to establish her coercive credentials clearly but without going to extremes in an effort to overcompensate. To do this she required a partner for three reasons. First, she needed a witness, someone who could judge her coercive performance and let her know that she had passed her tests. This gave her confidence. Second, she needed a partner to let it be known to other officers that she could be depended upon. This relieved her from having to prove herself repeatedly, to search for situations where she could demonstrate to others that she wasn't "soft," that she wouldn't crumble under pressure. This brought her acceptance and, ironically, the right to be "soft" when she thought it necessary. Finally, she needed a partner to experiment and learn from doing so. As she learned to coerce effectively she was bound to make mistakes for which her partner would have to compensate and cover. In turn she would be expected to do the same for him. From this interdependence and the inevitability of mistakes that would require analysis lest they should be repeated, the sanctuary of the patrol partnership became a place for talking through and working out the paradoxes and responsibilities of exercising coercive power.

Andy Renko, a thick-necked bull of a man and a good 'ol boy of slightly southern, slightly rural disposition, brings passion to his partnership with the urbane, reserved, and patient Bobby Hill. It is hard to imagine that anyone ever had a doubt about Renko's willingness to jump into the middle of things and mix it up if necessary. No question but what Renko is a take-charge guy. His problem is either that he is often not quite sure of what he is taking charge of or that when he is quite sure he is often wrong.

It is not that Andy Renko's doesn't have perspective, it is just that it is harder for him than for others to fit his experience into it. I suspect that some of this has to do with the willingness of the writers of *Hill Streets Blues* to subject Renko to a series of extraordinary problems that no one could be expected to keep in perspective. To wit: (1) after poor Renko's daddy died, his body was accidentally stolen and dumped into an alley where he was reprocessed as a sleeping wino; (2) Renko is faced with the problem of removing a full-grown steer from the upper floor of an urban housing project. (cattle, Renko finds, will willingly walk upstairs but categorically refuse to walk down); (3) after arresting a Caribbean woman, Renko finds himself the object of a voodoo curse, complete with doll and pins. I could go on describing Renko's extraordinary misadventures, but I won't. I am fairly confident that the writers of Hill Street will.

On a more mundane level, Renko's problems with perspective stem from a pre-police-career life experience in which the things he sees routinely on Hill Street just never happened. Renko is a downright decent, down home Southern boy policing a northern, urban, black and Hispanic ghetto. The people he polices *are* different from him. How could such a person not have problems putting his experiences into perspective?

The important thing to see about Renko is what it is that keeps him from distorting that very different world of Hill Street into "Us" and "Them" in the way Belker and Howard do. The secret is his love of talk, his willingness to open up on every topic that he doesn't understand, on every emotion that confuses him, on every action by himself or others that he failed to anticipate. To do this and to learn from it requires a place to talk and someone who has seen as much and knows more who is willing to listen and to tolerate mistakes. The sanctuary of a patrol partnership with Bobby Hill gives Renko this and more.

Neither Passion Nor Perspective: The Avoider: Jerry Fuchs.
Hill Street has only a few characters who lack both passion and perspective, who correspond to the type Muir calls the "avoider." One is Jerry Fuchs. He is a wreck of a man who is the former captain of a neighboring precinct. Fired in a corruption scandal, Fuchs now operates an equally corrupt but less lucrative private investigative service. Another is "Bad Sal" Benedetto whose corruption was discovered by Hill Street detectives. Bad Sal chose to take his life rather than go to jail. Such characters have played only brief parts in a few Hill Street episodes.

There are, however, some Hill Street regulars who have temporarily lapsed into avoider roles and subsequently recovered. Bobby Hill won a $100,000 lottery that so upended his personal life that he lost all perspective and passion until he squandered it. Johnny LaRue, a Hill Street detective, is an alcoholic who for a time was completely out control. He regained it one step short of dismissal. Avoiders do not seem to last very long on Hill Street. There is important work to be done there, and neither partners, fellow officers, nor supervisors will tolerate an officer who is unwilling to share the load or who interferes with other officers' efforts to carry it. This attitude of intolerance of corruption, avoidance, laziness, and incompetence on Hill Street is admirable. Let me turn now to those features of the Hill Street organizational environment which the third portion of Muir's general theory finds to make good police and good policing possible.

I now want to deal with three factors which seem to have fostered the development of . . . professionals. By way of shorthand, let us call the factors language, learning, and leadership. The first denotes an enjoyment of talk. The second refers to the skill of field sergeants in teaching the men of their squads on the job. The third points to the means available to a chief to affect inner perspectives and passions of the patrol men in his department [1977: 226].

LANGUAGE, LEARNING, AND LEADERSHIP

I have already said some things about the crucial role of talk to the development of police officers. The enjoyment of talk and the opportunity to talk privately played a key role in the development of two Hill Street police officers: Lucy Bates and Andy Renko. I have also tried to show that the disinclination to talk or the absence of a friend and police partner with whom to enjoy talk has taken its toll on the moral and intellectual development of Howard, Belker, and Henry. Having said this much about the importance of talk to the development of passion and perspective, I need to make only one more point about talk to emphasize the full range of its critical importance to Muir's theory of good police and good policing.

The point has to do with the role talk plays in the actual work of policing. The police officer's most important tool is his mouth. You will recall how important it was to Joe Wilkes in the family beef and to Bill Douglas in creating his firm and unflinching image. He used it to issue the warnings that would return the truant juveniles on his beat to a rational fearfulness. Although I described Mike Marshall's work on skid row briefly, you can probably imagine how crucial the kind of talk he engaged in—advice, counsel, warnings, cautions, humor, a kind word, an understanding conversation—was to "re-possession" of the dispossessed of skid row. The ability to talk in strong, subtle, and sensitive ways, the art of effective rhetoric is essential to the skillful exercise of coercion.

The fact is, however, that coercion, although it is the defining characteristic of the police role and the special and most paradoxical competence of police, is not the only means of controlling people. There are also exchange and persuasion. In fact, if we look back to the work of the Muir's three professional police officers—Marshall, Wilkes, and Douglas—it is not at all clear whether what each did with the people he policed is better described as "coercion" or as "exchange" or "persuasion." Certainly the work of Joe Wilkes in the family beef can easily be seen as persuading the warring couples to examine what they have and rediscover the value those once precious things might have again. Likewise, the work of Mike Marshall on skid row might well be understood as exchange. What he gave to the dispossessed he policed was a fair shake, decent treatment, understanding, someone they could count on, and even a small short-term loan when necessary. In exchange for these valuable gifts and services, they gave him the support he needed. Even the coercive work of Bill Douglas, whose task was to restore a rational fear into the minds of irresponsible youths, might better be understood as a carefully controlled act of persuasion rather than an exercise of coercive power.

The point I wish to make about these alternative interpretations of what happened on skid row, in the family beef, and with the irrational truant juveniles is a very simple one: The police officer's capacity to talk skillfully in terms the audience for those words will understand is as crucial to the use of exchange and persuasion as means of controlling people as it is to excercising coercive power.

For all these reasons Muir concludes, and I think rightly, that the development of good police and good policing cannot occur unless an atmosphere and environment is created in police agencies in which the skills and joys of talk are developed and encouraged. It is a conclusion with direct policy implications. The love of talk should be an attribute detected in prospective police applicants. It ought to be encouraged in police academies and required of new recruits. Officers with a love of talk should be selected to train police rookies and encourage them to learn to articulate what they think and feel. Patrol officers require partners for reasons that have nothing to do with danger to their bodies or their physical safety. To police alone and with no one to talk to places a patrol officer's mind and heart in jeopardy. A partner is essential for talking through the paradoxes of coercive power and working out a balance between moral passion and intellectual perspective. Finally, the encouragement of good talk by police supervisors and between police officers and their supervisors is an absolute necessity. In the next two sections, the first on learning and the second on leadership, I shall try to explain why.

Learning

After their partners, there is no one in any police department who is more important to the career, the development, the morale, and the daily life of patrol officers than their sergeant. Let's look at some choice words of the late, great Hill Street sergeant, Philip Freemason Esterhaus, to understand why that is. The scene is roll call, 7:01 a.m., and after a few perfunctory announcements Sgt. Esterhaus observes:

It has come to my attention that a certain group of ladies of less than pristine virtue and entreprenenural inclination have, of late, begun to satisfy a variety of appetites during the noon hour in the vicinity of Main and Poplar. As most of you know, a number of establishments at this location, including Ronald's Ribs and Mable's Table, already offer a midday repast which, despite its occasional shortcomings, attracts a sizable clientele from nearby industrial establishments. (Not to mention some stalwart members of this city's uniformed, public service.) It appears that with disturbing regularity a number of the private sector employees have begun to develop at this time of day a taste for certain delicacies to which Ronald and Mable are not equipped to cater. As the resulting financial loss to these and other restauranteurs in the environs will undoubtedly be passed along to steady customers in the form of higher prices or a further decrease in the quality of cuisine, it would be prudent of us to attempt to limit this new source of sumptuary competition. Officers Renko and Hill. It is my understanding that neither

of you are strangers to Mable's table. I wonder if I might entrust
you with this diplomatic mission?

What Esterhaus could have said was "We've been getting complaints of hookers working the lunch-hour crowd at Main and
Poplar Streets. Hill and Renko, move 'em out." He did not
because he had a lot more to say and the rhetorical capacity
to say it. Let's see what he *did* say.

What is important to note first about the situation is that
because Hill and Renko regularly eat at Mable's they should
have already noted and begun to take care of the traffic in
prostitution that has sprung up there. A point-blank instuction
to do so would have been the equivalent of a direct criticism
of Hill and Renko and, at roll call, a public one as well. It
would have put them on the defensive, obliged them to explain,
perhaps, that they had not been there recently or offer some
other type of excuse. But even insofar as it called for an explana-
tion it would have sponsored the impression that Esterhaus sus-
pected that they may not be doing their job. Any element of
criticism, suspicion, or mistrust of Hill and Renko was defused
by the humor with which Esterhaus presented the situation.

Second, the detail of Esterhaus's description left no doubt
in anyone's mind that he knew exactly what the situation was
at Main and Poplar. He knew that prostitution was a new
development in that locale at that time of day. He knew who
the clients were. He knew the principal complainants, the quality
of the food they served, and that Hill and Renko ate their
lunch there regularly. So while his message to Hill and Renko
was not read by them or anyone else in their platoon as criticism,
Esterhaus managed to communicate to one and all the fine
detail with which he knew the district and what the officers
who worked for him were and should be doing in it.

Third, the way in which Esterhaus presented the situation
not only specified what should be done about it but, even more
important, why it should be done and how. His words helped
officers in his platoon give meaning to what they were required
to do. And his description disarmed cynics and crusaders alike.
The prostitutes were not to be strong-armed off the street because
their behavior was immoral or because they threatened the virtue
of otherwise decent citizens. Esterhaus did not need to supply
his officers with a phoney moral passion. In the hierarchy of

things to become morally outraged about, Esterhaus communicated that prostitution should fall low on a Hill Street officer's list. This was a lesson to all who heard his roll call speech. His words kept prostitutes and prostitution in perspective. The women had to be moved because they were disturbing local businesses and local businesses had a right not to be disturbed in that way. It was at that level of emotion and with that level of understanding that Esterhaus wanted Hill and Renko to approach the women who were working the lunch trade at Main and Poplar and explain to them that they would have to take their business elsewhere.[1]

Finally, in the words he chose and the way he spoke, Esterhaus set an example that defied a widely popular and unflattering stereotype of police. The mark of Esterhaus's rhetoric was subtlety and delicacy, the opposites of crudeness. His speech assumed that the officers in his squad were intelligent enough to understand anything within reason. Once he had communicated that, he could then go on to expect it of them.

Obviously, it is not possible to express all the ways a sergeant can influence the careers, development, morale, and daily life of officers under his command from this one speech by Esterhaus. Sergeants make up work schedules, arrange days off, conduct inspections, write up annual evaluations of each officer's work, dispense job assignments, and support or discourage transfers within the department. All of these powers which profoundly influence the lives of patrol officers are used by sergeants to teach those who work for them not only what is expected but how and in exactly what terms those expectations should be understood. A great sergeant can make a patrol officer's life a joy. A lousy sergeant can make it sheer misery.

Leadership

Unlike their sergeant, the leader of a police agency, a chief, a captain, or a commander of a district has very little direct influence over the daily lives of patrol officers. Chiefs, captains, or commanders cannot promote or give raises; administratively they are too far away from the daily work of patrol officers to know the routine stuff of which their working days consist. Except, that is, on those occasions when some incident consists of an event that might lead to scandal. The scandal or the possibility of one is virtually the only occasion when the top leadership of a police agency becomes directly involved in street-level police work.

Indirectly, and sometimes in ways patrol officers never see, a top police administrator could affect the patrol officer's lot. Largely this is a matter of deflecting, defining, or focusing the external influences that play upon a police agency. The press, politicians, powerful individual citizens, interest groups, police unions, other police administrators, and other divisions of the police department all have claims and agendas which they expect a top police administrator to observe. No administrator can satisfy all of these conflicting interests, but none of them can be ignored because each is a powerful person or represents a powerful group. Furthermore, in choosing which of these insisting masters to serve and which to serve at another master's expense, the choice cannot be made merely in terms of which of them commands the most power at the moment. It is the mark of the good police administrator to understand that while in the short run it is necessary to survive, in the long run he is held hostage by his troops.

Frank's Choices

Let's examine an incident in which the man in command of Hill Street, Captain Frank Furillo, is called upon to deal directly with a street-level police problem. The incident is from an episode that appeared in the first week of October 1984.

It was a hostage situation. The victimizer, who was armed and firing at police who had surrounded the building, had barracaded himself in a second floor apartment. He was threatening to kill his hostage, and attempts by Henry to negotiate with him had failed. When it looked as if he might carry through on his threat, Howard ordered the EATers to shoot tear gas into the room to drive him to window and, they hoped, away from his hostage. When he appeared at the window he was alone, screaming threats, and brandishing a rifle. Howard gave the order to shoot him, but just as Howard did the man slumped over into the window ledge and dropped his weapon to the street, apparently overcome by the effects of the gas. A split-second later, and before Howard had rescinded his order to cease fire, one of the EATers shot and killed the man. Just after he had fired his weapon and saw that he had hit his mark, the young EATer exclaimed, "Gotcha, you son of a bitch!" The entire incident was recorded by a television crew. What are Captain Frank Furillo's choices in handling this incident and how would those choices go on to influence police and policing on Hill Street? Line police officers and citizens tend to think of situations like the one Frank faced as presenting only two real options. For the public, and especially a public presented with such a vivid display of real violence and an officer's subsequent profane celebration of it, the possibilities appear to be that the department would either cover up the scandal or dismiss the brutal, bloodthirsty officer and give him the punishment he deserves. For line police officers, who appreciated the possibility that they might someday be in a similar situation, the choices appeared to be whether the top administration and particularly Furillo would back them up or sell them out. Leaning toward the public's perspective on the situation is the press, which, after all, possessed the crucial evidence of the outrageous offense, and the chief of the department, who knows that the scandal could be defused fairly quickly at the cost of just one EATer.

What Frank knew was that the situation was far more complicated than it appeared to any of these outside observers. For one thing, Howard was not prepared to let one of his EATers take the heat alone. He pointed out, quite correctly, that it was he who had given the order to fire on the hostage taker, and he had not rescinded that command before his youthful EATer opened fire. Although Howard privately conceded to Frank that the young officer should have waited when he saw the weapon drop from the hostage taker's hand, Howard was prepared to testify at a trial that the young officer was following his explicit orders to shoot when he did. Actually Howard did not rescind the order because things happened so quickly that he did not have the time to do so. Howard's point raised the possibility that the young EATer might have thought that Howard did not rescind the order for some reason of which the young officer was unaware.

Both Howard and Frank also know that in the heat of combat officers say things that should not be read as true indicators of what they are inside. It is the responsibility of a police officer to keep such emotions under control, but in a young officer in his early twenties who had for the first time in his life just shot and killed a man, a lapse like this might be forgiven. Up to the moment of the incident in question the young officer had shown himself to be a fine young policeman.

Frank and Howard knew as well that the young EATer was already suffering severely for his act. Each time the tape was run on television, he was portrayed before the entire city as a man who loved to kill. He had received a call from his mother, who saw a tape of the incident. She asked him how he could have done such a horrible thing. Howard attempted to get the young officer to talk to him about the incident, but the young man, deeply upset, refused to do so. It was Howard's contention that if this young man were found guilty by a police trial board and punished for his act, it would ruin him forever as a police officer and possibly even as a man.

Howard asked Frank to intercede in behalf of the young officer in the impending Internal Affairs investigation of the incident. As Howard saw it, Internal Affairs was an arm of the chief. The chief, in Howard's opinion, was a slave of the media. Thus, an Internal Affairs investigation of the incident would simply turn out to be nothing more than a media lynching.

There was, however, still more to the story than Howard realized or was prepared to argue. The public as well as police officers had repeatedly been shown an incident in which a Hill Street officer came off as a bloodthirsty killer. That impression was strong enough, you will remember, to raise doubt in, if not convince even the young officer's own mother. There was even reason to believe that the young officer was beginning to suspect this bloodthirstiness of himself. Moreover, even if there were some police officers who were willing to see the incident as a faulty, split-second decision marred by an understandable outburst in the heat of the moment, Frank knew that there were also officers who were happy when the "son of bitch" did get "blown away." The public had a right to know that its police were not bloodthirsty killers and would not allow such a person to remain in their ranks. Likewise, the department had an obligation to teach those officers who were inclined to cheer the young EATer's act that the department would not tolerate that kind of behavior. To teach this critical lesson to an outraged public as well as to officers inclined to violence, might it not be worth it, in both the short and the long run, to make a severe example of the young EATer?

Ultimately this may be the fate of the young EATer. But, at present, Frank made two decisions that suggest that it may not be. First, he refused Howard's request to influence the Internal Affairs investigation. Had he done so his interference would have confirmed that the investigation was part of the chief's plan to "crucify" the young officer. In fact the investigation cleared the officer of wrongdoing, although it found him guilty of poor judgment.

Second, Frank leaked the findings of the Internal Affairs investigation to a newspaper reporter in advance of their release by the chief. In part, he did so in exchange for an understanding with the reporter that the reporter would write a fair account of the incident. Frank did not request a whitewash or a coverup in exchange for the information, merely a fair and honest account. What he hoped for was a story that might go deeply enough into the realities of the incident to give the public, police, and the young EATer a sense of perspective.

But, I suspect, he also leaked the information for an altogether different reason. By doing so he hoped to prevent the chief from changing the findings of the investigation. Frank knows that in this situation there is a distinct possibility that the chief would choose to sacrifice the unfortunate young EATer for both the long and short run good of the department. The chief, Frank also knows, is a man of passion, if not perspective.

I do not know how the writers of *Hill Street Blues* will conclude this incident. As I write this they have not done so and it does not really matter how they do. The fate of the young EATer is inconsequential because after all we have said about him, and all the other characters of Hill Street, he and they are only illusions. If they have any value whatsoever, it is as models to help think through the idea of police. They have helped me do so and I hope the same is true for you.

DISCUSSION QUESTIONS

Let me leave you with some questions for discussion and a bit of advice which may sustain their illusion a bit longer.

1. Should Frank have leaked the findings of the Internal Affairs investigation to the press?

2. Should he have undercut the chief's option to reverse the Internal Affairs investigation's findings?

3. Should the chief punish Frank if he found out that he was the one that leaked the information to the press?

4. Should the chief sacrifice the young EATer in the long- or short-term interests of the department?

5. Should the chief do so if the young EATer's unfortunate experience had already damaged him enough to destroy his potential for ever becoming a good policeman?

6. Do you think you could police or govern justly *and* innocently?

Be very, very careful out there.

NOTES

1. The speech is an outright forgery. I made the whole thing up myself and falsely attributed it to Phil Esterhaus. I feel no guilt for having done so because I am absolutely certain that he could have said it and would have said it, though perhaps more eloquently, if he had the chance. I would have used a real Esterhaus speech, and there are many that would have served my purpose equally as well, but I do not have scripts or tapes of the show, only a fond memory of his character and an ear for his distinctive rhetorical style.

REFERENCES

ALLEN, R. J. (1976) "The police and substantive rulemaking: reconciling principle and expediency." University of Pennsylvania Law Review 125, 1.

ARCHULETA, A. O. (1974) "Police discretion v. plea bargaining." The Police Chief (April).

ARENDT, H. (1973) "On violence," in Crises of the Republic. Harmondsworth, England: Penguin.

AUDEN, W. H. (1956) "The guilty vicarage," pp. 146-158 in The Dyer's Hand and Other Essays. New York: Alfred A. Knopf.

BITTNER, E. (1980) The Functions of Police in Modern Society. Cambridge, MA: Oelgeschlager, Gunn & Hain.

———(1974) "Florence Nightingale in pursuit of Willie Sutton: a theory of police," pp. 17-44 in H. Jacob (ed.) The Potential for Reform of Criminal Justice. Beverly Hills, CA: Sage.

BLACK, D. (1971) "The social organization of arrest." Stanford Law Review 23 (June).

BROWN, M. K. (1981) Working the Street: Police Discretion and the Dilemmas of Reform. New York: Russell Sage.

BROWN, R. M. (1969) "The American vigilante tradition," pp. 121-169 in H. D. Graham and T. R. Gurr (eds.) Violence in America: Historical and Comparative Perspectives. Washington, DC: Government Printing Office.

———(1975) Strain of Violence: Historical Studies of American Violence and Vigilantism. Oxford: Oxford University Press.

CAWELTI, J. G. (1976) Adventure, Mystery, and Romance. Chicago: University of Chicago Press.

CHAIKEN, J., P. GREENWOOD, and J. PETERSILLIA (1977) "The criminal investigation process: a summary report." Policy Analysis 3, 2: 187-217.

CHANDLER, R. (1972) "The simple art of murder," pp. 1-22 in The Simple Art of Murder. New York: Ballatine.

COBB, B. (1957) The First Detectives and the Early Career of Richard Mayne, Commissioner of Police. London: Faber and Faber.

CRITCHLEY, T. A. (1967) A History of Police in England and Wales. Montclair, NJ: Patterson Smith.

CUMMING, E., I. CUMMING, and L. EDELL (1965) "Policeman as philosopher, guide, and friend." Social Forces 12.

DAVIS, K. C. (1969) Discretionary Justice. Baton Rouge: Louisiana State University Press.

———(1975) Police Discretion. St. Paul. MN: West.

DOUTHIT, N. (1975) "August Vollmer: Berkley's first chief of police and the emergence of police professionalism." California Historical Quarterly 54 (Spring): 101-124.

DURHAM, P. (1963) Down These Mean Streets a Man Must Go: Raymond Chandler's Knight. Chapel Hill: University of North Carolina Press.

FOGELSON, R. (1977) Big City Police. Cambridge, MA: Harvard University Press.

FRANKLIN, J. H. (1969) From Slavery to Freedom. New York: Random House.

GARDINER, J. A. (1969) Traffic and the Police. Cambridge, MA: Harvard University Press.

GASH, N. (1961) Mr. Secretary Peel. Cambridge, MA: Harvard University Press.

GOLDSTEIN, H. (1977) Policing a Free Society. Cambridge, MA: Ballinger.

GOLDSTEIN, J. (1960) "Police discretion not to invoke the criminal justice process: low visibility decisions in the administration of justice." Yale Law Journal 69 (March): 543-594.

GORER, G. (1955) Exploring English Character. London: Cresset.

GREENBERG, B. et al. (1972) Enhancement of the Investigative Function. Menlo Park, CA: Stanford Research Institute.

HALLER, M. (1976) "Historical roots of police behavior: Chicago 1890-1925." Law and Society Review 10, 2: 303-323.

HAYCRAFT, H. [ed.] (1946) The Art of the Mystery Story: A Collection of Critical Essays. New York: Simon & Schuster.

HOWSON, G. (1970) Thief-Taker General: The Rise and Fall of Jonathan Wild. London: Hutchinson.

HUNT, I. C. and B. Cohen (1971) Minority Recruiting in the New York City Police Department. Santa Monica, CA: Rand Corp.

Institute for Defense Analysis (1967) Task Force Report: Science and Technology. Report of the President's Commission on Law Enforcement and the Administration of Justice. Washington, DC: Government Printing Office.

Kansas City Police Department (1971) Survey of Municipal Police Departments. Kansas City: Author.

KELLING, G. et al. (1974) The Kansas City Preventive Patrol Experiment: A Technical Report. Washington, DC: The Police Foundation.

KLOCKARS, C. B. (1983) Thinking about Police. New York: McGraw-Hill.

———(1980) "Jonathan Wild and the modern sting," pp. 225-260 in J. A. Inciardi and C. E. Faupel (eds.) History and Crime: Implications for Criminal Justice Policy. Beverly Hills, CA: Sage.

LANE, R. (1967) Policing the City: Boston 1822-1885. Cambridge, MA: Harvard University Press.

LEE, M. (1971) A History of Police in England. Montclair, NJ: Patterson Smith.

LUNDMAN, R. J. (1979) "Organizational norms and police discretion: an observational study of police work with traffic law violators." Criminology 17 (August): 159-171.

MADDEN, D. [ed.] (1968) Tough Guy Writers of the Thirties. Carbondale: Southern Illinois University Press.

MILLER, W. (1977) Cops and Bobbies. Chicago: University of Chicago Press.

MORRIS, W. A. (1910) The Frankpledge System. New York: Longmans Green.

MUIR, W. K. (1977) Police: Streetcorner Politicians. Chicago: University of Chicago Press.

MURCH, A. E. (1958) The Development of the Detective Novel. New York: Philosophical Library.

National Advisory Commission on Civil Disorders (1968) Report of the National Advisory Commission on Civil Disorders. Washington, DC: Government Printing Office.

National Crime Survey (1977) Washington, DC: Government Printing Office.

NEVINS, F. M., Jr. [ed.] (1970) The Mystery Writer's Art. Bowling Green, OH: Bowling Green University Popular Press.

OUSBY, I. (1976) Bloodhounds of Heaven. Cambridge, MA: Harvard University Press.

The Police Foundation (1981) Newark Foot Patrol Experiment. Washington, DC: Author.

PRINGLE, P. (1958) The Thief Takers. London: Museum Press.

———(1965) Hue and Cry. New York: William Morrow.

RADZINOWICZ, L. (1948-1957) History of the English Criminal Law, Vols. 1-4. New York: Macmillan.

———(1957) A History of the English Criminal Law and Its Administration from 1750 (Vol. 1). New York: Macmillan.

REISS, A. J., Jr. (1974) "Discretionary justice," in D. Glaser (ed.) Handbook of Criminology. Chicago: Rand McNally.

———(1971) The Police and the Public. New Haven, CT: Yale University Press.

RICHARDSON, J. F. (1970) The New York Police: Colonial Times to 1901. New York: Oxford University Press.

RUEHLMAN, W. (1974) Saint with a Gun: The Unlawful American Private Eye. New York: New York University Press.

SPELMAN, W. G. and D. K. BROWN (1983) "Response time," pp. 160-166 in C. B. Klockars (ed.) Thinking About Police. New York: McGraw-Hill.

THEOHARRIS, A. G. (1978) Spying on Americans. Philadelphia: Temple University Press.

TOBIAS, J. J. (1967) Crime and Industrial Society in the Nineteenth Century. London: Batsford.

UNGER, S. J. (1976) FBI. Boston: Little, Brown.

WEBB, S. and B. WEBB (1906) English Local Government from the Revolution to the Municipal Corporations Act: The Parish and the County. London: Longmans Green.

WEBER, M. (1948) "Class, status, and party," in H. Gerth and C. Wright Mills (eds. and trans.) From Max Weber. New York: Oxford University Press.

ZERUBAVEL, E. (1981) Hidden Rhythms. Chicago: University of Chicago Press.

INDEX